# Berlin at Christmas

*A Festive Travel Guide to the City's Markets, Lights, and Attractions, Plus Tips for a Stress-Free Holiday Trip in 2024*

**PEREGRINE ASHFORD**

# TABLE OF CONTENTS

# Preface

As the first snowflakes of December drifted gently onto the cobblestone streets, Berlin transformed into a city of wonder and enchantment. The air was crisp, tinged with the sweet scent of roasted chestnuts and the warm, spiced aroma of Glühwein. In the heart of the city, under the towering shadow of the Brandenburg Gate, twinkling lights began to flicker to life, illuminating Berlin in a golden glow that could melt even the coldest of hearts.

Amidst this magical transformation, a young traveler named Clara found herself stepping off the train at Hauptbahnhof, her breath visible in the frigid air. She had come to Berlin on a whim, driven by stories of its Christmas markets, legendary for their charm and splendor. But what Clara discovered was far more than she had ever imagined.

Her first stop was the Gendarmenmarkt Christmas Market, a place where history and holiday cheer blended seamlessly. As she wandered through the market, Clara marveled at the exquisite craftsmanship on display—delicate glass ornaments, hand-carved wooden toys, and intricate lacework that seemed almost too perfect to touch. The market buzzed with the laughter of children and the hum of festive music, creating a symphony of joy that wrapped around her like a warm embrace.

Drawn by the aroma of freshly baked pastries, Clara found herself at a stall selling Lebkuchen, the traditional German gingerbread. The vendor, an elderly man with a twinkle in his eye, handed her a heart-shaped piece wrapped in bright red ribbon. "For good luck," he said with a smile. As she bit into the sweet, spiced treat, Clara felt a wave of warmth that seemed to chase away the winter chill. The city, with its sparkling lights and festive spirit, began to feel like home.

The days passed in a blur of wonder. Clara explored the grand Charlottenburg Palace Market, where the baroque architecture served as a stunning backdrop to the festive stalls. She sipped hot chocolate while watching ice skaters glide gracefully across a rink set up in the palace gardens, their laughter mingling with the soft strains of classical music drifting through the air.

But it was the night she stumbled upon the Christmas Market at Alexanderplatz that truly captured her heart. The market was alive with energy, a bustling hub where locals and tourists alike gathered to celebrate the season. Clara joined in the fun, riding the Ferris wheel that offered a breathtaking view of the city bathed in the glow of Christmas lights. As the wheel slowly turned, Berlin's skyline stretched out before her, a dazzling array of colors and lights that seemed to dance in the winter night.

At the top, as the wheel paused to allow passengers to take in the view, Clara looked out over the city and felt a profound sense of peace. Below her, the market bustled with life, but up here, all was quiet, save for the distant sound of a Christmas choir singing a hymn that floated up to meet her. In that moment, she understood why Berlin was often called the heart of Christmas in Europe.

It wasn't just the markets, the lights, or the festivities that made Berlin special during the holiday season. It was the way the city seemed to invite everyone—locals, tourists, young and old—into its warm embrace, offering them a place to belong, even if only for a few fleeting days.

As the Ferris wheel began its descent, Clara felt a tear slip down her cheek, not from sadness, but from the overwhelming beauty of it all. She realized that Berlin had given her more than just a holiday experience; it had given her a memory that she would cherish forever.

And so, as she stepped off the Ferris wheel and made her way back through the market, her heart swelled with a quiet joy. The city had cast its spell on her, just as it had on countless others before her. Berlin at Christmas was not just a destination—it was a feeling, a magic that lingered long after the last snowflake had melted away.

As Clara returned to her hotel that night, she knew one thing for certain: she would return to Berlin again. For in this city, amidst the twinkling lights and the soft hum of holiday cheer, she had found a place where the spirit of Christmas lived, not just in the markets and the decorations, but in the hearts of all who wandered its winter streets.

# Introduction

Welcome to the enchanting world of Berlin at Christmas, where tradition meets modernity in a city that transforms into a winter wonderland each December. Berlin, Germany's vibrant capital, is renowned for its rich history, cutting-edge culture, and dynamic art scene. However, during the Christmas season, the city takes on a unique character, blending its historic charm with festive cheer, making it one of the most magical destinations in Europe.

This travel guide is your companion to exploring Berlin during this most wonderful time of the year. Whether you're a seasoned traveler or visiting Berlin for the first time, this guide will help you discover the best of the city's Christmas markets, light displays, seasonal attractions, and culinary delights. We will provide you with practical tips for navigating the city, making the most of your time, and ensuring a stress-free holiday experience. So, wrap yourself in a cozy scarf, grab a cup of hot cocoa, and let's embark on a journey through the heart of Berlin at Christmas.

## Why Berlin at Christmas?

Berlin is a city that wears many hats, and each one is as fascinating as the last. From its storied past as the epicenter of European history to its modern reputation as a hub of creativity and innovation, Berlin never fails to captivate. But it's during the Christmas season that

Berlin truly comes alive, offering an experience that is both heartwarming and awe-inspiring.

One of the primary reasons why Berlin stands out as a Christmas destination is its remarkable array of Christmas markets. These markets, known as Weihnachtsmärkte, are scattered throughout the city, each offering a unique atmosphere, local crafts, and delicious food and drink. From the grand and historic Gendarmenmarkt to the eclectic and quirky Weihnachtsrodeo in Kreuzberg, Berlin's Christmas markets cater to every taste and preference. The tradition of these markets dates back to the Middle Ages, and today they are a testament to the city's ability to blend the old with the new, the traditional with the modern.

But Berlin at Christmas is not just about markets. The city's architecture, already impressive throughout the year, becomes even more magnificent as it is adorned with festive lights and decorations. Streets like Kurfürstendamm and Unter den Linden are transformed into glittering boulevards, while iconic landmarks such as the Brandenburg Gate and Berlin Cathedral are illuminated in ways that highlight their grandeur. Berlin's light displays are nothing short of spectacular, making the city a feast for the eyes and a dream for photographers.

Another reason to visit Berlin during the Christmas season is its diverse range of seasonal attractions and events. From ice skating rinks to holiday concerts, from festive performances at the city's renowned theaters to special exhibitions at its world-class museums, Berlin offers something for everyone. The city's cultural calendar is packed with activities that will immerse you in the spirit of the season, whether you're travellng alone, with a partner, or with family.

For those who love culinary adventures, Berlin is a gastronomic paradise, especially during Christmas. The city's Christmas markets offer a wide variety of traditional German treats, from Bratwurst and Glühwein to Lebkuchen and Stollen. But Berlin's food scene is not limited to tradition. The city's diverse population means that you can also find international holiday dishes, whether you're in the mood for Italian, French, or Scandinavian Christmas fare. In Berlin, the festive season is an opportunity to indulge in flavors from around the world while enjoying the warm hospitality of local cafes and restaurants.

Moreover, Berlin is an excellent base for exploring other parts of Germany during the Christmas season. The city's central location and excellent transport connections make it easy to take day trips to other enchanting destinations, such as Potsdam, Dresden, or the Harz Mountains, each offering its own unique holiday charm. Whether you're looking to explore palaces, attend Christmas markets in smaller towns, or experience the beauty of Germany's winter landscapes, Berlin provides the perfect starting point.

Finally, Berlin's spirit of inclusivity and diversity ensures that everyone feels welcome during the Christmas season. Whether you're celebrating with loved ones or on a solo adventure, Berlin offers a sense of belonging and warmth that is truly special. The city's rich history of resilience and openness is reflected in its Christmas celebrations, which embrace people of all backgrounds and traditions. In Berlin, Christmas is not just a holiday; it's a celebration of community, connection, and the joy of shared experiences.

## How to Use This Guide

This travel guide is designed to be your comprehensive resource for exploring Berlin at Christmas. Whether you're planning a short visit or an extended stay, the information provided here will help you make the most of your time in the city. To ensure that you have a seamless and enjoyable experience, the guide is organized into easy-to-navigate sections, each focusing on a different aspect of Berlin's Christmas offerings.

**1. Discovering Berlin's Christmas Markets:** This section provides detailed information about Berlin's most popular and unique Christmas markets. You'll find descriptions of each market's atmosphere, what to expect in terms of food, drinks, and crafts, as well as practical tips for navigating the markets, such as the best times to visit and how to avoid crowds. Whether you're looking for a traditional experience or something more offbeat, this section will help you choose the markets that best suit your interests.

**2. Illuminating Berlin: Christmas Lights and Decorations:** Berlin's festive light displays are a highlight of the season, and this section will guide you to the best spots in the city to see them. From iconic streets to grand buildings, you'll discover where to find the most stunning light installations. The section also includes photography tips for capturing the magic of Berlin at night, ensuring that you can take home memories of the city's holiday splendor.

**3. Must-See Winter Attractions in Berlin:** In addition to its Christmas markets, Berlin is home to a wide range of winter attractions that are especially enchanting during the holiday season. This section covers everything from historical sites with a festive twist to family-friendly activities and cultural highlights. Whether you're interested in exploring Berlin's rich history or enjoying a day of ice skating, this section has you covered.

**4. Culinary Delights: Savoring Berlin's Festive Flavors:** Berlin's Christmas season is a time for indulgence, and this section introduces you to the city's culinary delights. You'll learn about traditional German holiday dishes, discover where to find the best cafes and restaurants for a cozy Christmas meal, and even get tips on international holiday cuisine available in Berlin. Whether you're a foodie or simply looking for a warm place to relax, this section will guide you to the best spots to enjoy Berlin's festive flavors.

**5. Shopping in Berlin: From Luxury to Local Crafts:** If you're looking to do some Christmas shopping while in Berlin, this section is for you. It covers the city's top shopping destinations, from luxury department stores to local artisan markets. You'll also find information on tax-free shopping, gift wrapping services, and where to find unique souvenirs to take home. Whether you're searching for high-end fashion or handmade crafts, this section will help you find the perfect gifts for your loved ones.

**6. Experiencing Berlin's Winter Wonderland Outdoors:** Berlin's parks and outdoor spaces are just as enchanting in winter as they are in summer. This section guides you to the best outdoor winter activities, from ice skating to winter walks in snow-covered parks. You'll also find information on guided tours that will help you explore Berlin's winter wonderland in depth. If you love the outdoors, this section will inspire you to bundle up and experience Berlin's natural beauty during the holiday season.

**7. Staying Stress-Free During the Holidays in Berlin:** Traveling during the holidays can be stressful, but this section is designed to help you stay relaxed and enjoy your time in Berlin. It offers practical advice on everything from planning your trip to avoiding crowds and staying safe and warm. You'll also find tips on navigating Berlin's public transport system and making the most of your visit, ensuring that your holiday in Berlin is as stress-free as possible.

**8. Family Fun: Kid-Friendly Activities in Berlin:** If you're traveling with children, this section will help you find the best kid-friendly activities in Berlin. From interactive museums to festive events for families, you'll discover plenty of options to keep your little ones entertained. The section also includes indoor activities for when the weather gets too cold, ensuring that your family has a memorable and enjoyable holiday in Berlin.

**9. Unforgettable Day Trips from Berlin:** Berlin is an excellent base for exploring other parts of Germany, and this section highlights some of the best day trips you can take during the Christmas season. Whether you're interested in visiting the historic city of Potsdam, exploring Dresden's Christmas markets, or enjoying winter sports in the Harz Mountains, this section provides all the information you need to plan your excursions. Each destination offers its own unique holiday charm, making these day trips a perfect addition to your Berlin adventure.

Throughout the guide, you'll find practical tips and insider information that will help you make the most of your time in Berlin. Whether you're looking for hidden gems, the best times to visit popular attractions, or recommendations for off-the-beaten-path experiences, this guide has you covered. Our goal is to provide you with a comprehensive resource that not only informs but also inspires you to experience the magic of Berlin at Christmas to its fullest.

# Overview of Berlin's Holiday Spirit

Berlin's holiday spirit is a reflection of the city's unique character—a blend of tradition, creativity, and a deep sense of community. During the Christmas season, this spirit is on full display, as Berliners and visitors alike come together to celebrate the joy and warmth of the season in a city that is as diverse as it is welcoming.

One of the defining features of Berlin's holiday spirit is its inclusivity. The city is known for its openness and acceptance, and this is particularly evident during the Christmas season. Berlin's Christmas markets, for example, are not just places to shop and eat; they are spaces where people from all walks of life can come together and share in the festive atmosphere. Whether you're a local or a visitor, young or old, Berlin's Christmas markets offer a sense of belonging and connection that is truly special.

The diversity of Berlin's population is also reflected in the city's holiday celebrations. While traditional German Christmas customs are a central part of the festivities, you'll also find influences from other cultures and traditions. This is particularly evident in the food offerings at the Christmas markets, where alongside Bratwurst and Glühwein, you can find international holiday treats from countries like Italy, France, and Scandinavia. Berlin's multiculturalism adds a richness and depth to the holiday season, making it a time to celebrate not just Christmas, but the many ways in which people around the world mark the end of the year.

Berlin's holiday spirit is also characterized by its creativity. The city has long been a center of artistic innovation, and this is reflected in the way Berliners celebrate Christmas. From the stunning light installations that adorn the city's streets to the creative markets that offer unique handmade gifts, Berlin is a city that knows how to celebrate in style. This creativity extends to the many events and performances that take place during the holiday season, whether it's a modern twist on a classic Christmas concert or an avant-garde theater production with a festive theme. In Berlin, the holiday season is a time to celebrate not just tradition, but also the new and the innovative.

Community plays a central role in Berlin's holiday spirit. The city has a strong tradition of coming together to support those in need, and this is particularly evident during the Christmas season. Many of the city's Christmas markets, for example, donate a portion of their proceeds to charity, and you'll find numerous opportunities to participate in charitable events, from donation drives to volunteer opportunities. Berlin's holiday season is not just about enjoying the festivities; it's also about giving back and supporting the community.

The spirit of resilience is another important aspect of Berlin's holiday season. The city has a long and complex history, marked by periods of division and hardship. But Berlin has always emerged stronger, and this resilience is reflected in the way the city celebrates Christmas. The festive season in Berlin is a time to come together, to reflect on the past, and to look forward to the future with hope and optimism. This sense of resilience and renewal is a key part of what makes Berlin's holiday spirit so special.

Finally, Berlin's holiday spirit is about joy. Despite the cold weather, Berliners embrace the winter season with warmth and enthusiasm. The city's Christmas markets are filled with laughter and music, its streets are alive with the sound of holiday cheer, and its cafes and restaurants are cozy havens where people gather to enjoy good food, good company, and the simple pleasures of the season. In Berlin, Christmas is a time to slow down, to appreciate the beauty of the city in winter, and to find joy in the little things.

# Chapter 1: Discovering Berlin's Christmas Markets

Berlin's Christmas markets are legendary, offering a unique blend of history, culture, and festive cheer. These markets, known as Weihnachtsmärkte, are an essential part of the holiday season in Germany, and Berlin hosts some of the most enchanting ones in the country. They are more than just places to shop; they are vibrant social hubs where people gather to celebrate the season, enjoy traditional foods and drinks, and experience the magic of Christmas in a way that is both timeless and contemporary.

In this chapter, we will explore three of Berlin's most beloved traditional Christmas markets: the Gendarmenmarkt Christmas Market, Charlottenburg Palace Market, and Spandau Christmas Market. Each of these markets has its own unique charm and atmosphere, offering visitors a chance to experience Berlin's holiday spirit in different ways.

## 1.1 Traditional Markets to Explore

### Gendarmenmarkt Christmas Market

Nestled in the heart of Berlin's historic center, the Gendarmenmarkt Christmas Market is often regarded as one of the most beautiful in the city. The market is set against the stunning backdrop of the Gendarmenmarkt square, flanked by the grand architecture of the

Französischer Dom (French Cathedral), the Deutscher Dom (German Cathedral), and the Konzerthaus (Concert Hall). This picturesque setting alone makes the market worth a visit, but it's the atmosphere and offerings that truly make it special.

**History and Atmosphere:**
The Gendarmenmarkt Christmas Market has a long-standing tradition and is one of the most popular markets in Berlin. Its reputation is built on its elegant ambiance and high-quality offerings. As you enter the market, you are greeted by the soft glow of thousands of twinkling lights, the scent of mulled wine, and the sound of holiday music. The market's layout is carefully designed to guide visitors through a journey of festive discovery, with each stall offering something unique.

**What to Expect:**
The Gendarmenmarkt Christmas Market is known for its artisanal crafts and gourmet food. Here, you'll find an array of stalls selling handmade gifts, including intricate wood carvings, delicate glass ornaments, and beautifully crafted jewelry. Many of the artisans are local, and their work reflects the rich cultural heritage of Berlin and Germany.

In addition to shopping, the market offers a culinary experience that is hard to beat. Gourmet food stalls serve up a variety of traditional German treats, such as Bratwurst, Raclette, and Kartoffelpuffer (potato pancakes). For those with a sweet tooth, there are plenty of options, from freshly baked Lebkuchen (gingerbread) to warm, sugary Kaiserschmarrn (Austrian-style shredded pancakes). Of course, no visit to a German Christmas market would be complete without a cup of Glühwein, the spiced mulled wine that is synonymous with the hollday season.

The market also features a variety of entertainment, including live performances of Christmas carols, classical music, and dance. The central stage in the market often hosts choirs, orchestras, and even acrobats, creating a festive atmosphere that is both lively and refined. The combination of high-quality crafts, gourmet food, and cultural performances makes the Gendarmenmarkt Christmas Market a must-visit destination for anyone looking to experience the magic of Berlin at Christmas.

**Practical Tips:**
The Gendarmenmarkt Christmas Market is open from late November until just after Christmas, typically closing on December 31st. The market can get very crowded, especially in the evenings and on weekends, so it's a good idea to visit during the day if you prefer a more relaxed experience. There is a small entrance fee, which helps maintain the high quality of the market and its offerings. Be sure to dress warmly, as the market is outdoors and Berlin's winter can be quite chilly.

### Charlottenburg Palace Market

For a Christmas market experience that combines history, elegance, and festive charm, look no further than the Charlottenburg Palace Market. Located in the western part of Berlin, this market is set against the stunning backdrop of Charlottenburg Palace, one of the city's most beautiful and historically significant buildings. The palace, with its Baroque architecture and expansive gardens, provides a fairy-tale setting for a Christmas market that feels both grand and intimate.

**History and Atmosphere:**
The Charlottenburg Palace Market is relatively young compared to other traditional markets in Berlin, but it has quickly become one of the city's most beloved. The market takes full advantage of its location, with the palace and its gardens illuminated by thousands of lights, creating a magical atmosphere that transports visitors to a winter wonderland. The market's layout is spacious, with wide paths that allow visitors to stroll leisurely among the stalls while taking in the stunning views of the palace.

**What to Expect:**
The Charlottenburg Palace Market offers a wide variety of stalls, each housed in charming wooden huts that add to the market's traditional feel. The focus here is on high-quality, handcrafted goods, with many vendors offering unique items that make perfect gifts or souvenirs. From hand-knitted scarves and hats to

intricately designed Christmas ornaments, the market has something for everyone.

In addition to its shopping opportunities, the Charlottenburg Palace Market is known for its exceptional food and drink. The market offers a wide range of traditional German holiday foods, including Grünkohl (kale stew), roasted chestnuts, and Raclette. For dessert, visitors can indulge in treats like Marzipan, roasted almonds, and Stollen (German Christmas cake). There are also plenty of options for hot drinks to keep you warm as you explore the market, including Glühwein, hot chocolate, and Eierpunsch (a German version of eggnog).

One of the highlights of the Charlottenburg Palace Market is its ice skating rink, which is set up in the palace gardens. Skating under the twinkling lights with the palace as your backdrop is an unforgettable experience that captures the joy and beauty of the holiday season. The market also offers a range of entertainment options, including live music, performances by local choirs, and activities for children, such as carousel rides and puppet shows.

**Practical Tips:**
The Charlottenburg Palace Market typically opens in late November and runs until just before Christmas. The market is open in the evenings, with extended hours on weekends, making it a perfect place to visit after a day of sightseeing. The palace itself is worth a visit, and

many visitors choose to explore the palace during the day and then enjoy the market in the evening. The market is family-friendly, with plenty of activities to keep children entertained, and there is no entrance fee, although donations are appreciated.

**Spandau Christmas Market**

For a truly traditional Christmas market experience, head to the Spandau Christmas Market, located in the charming historic district of Spandau in western Berlin. This market is one of the largest in Berlin and is known for its authentic, old-world atmosphere. The market spreads throughout the picturesque streets of Spandau's Altstadt (Old Town), offering visitors a chance to experience a Christmas market that feels both timeless and full of life.

**History and Atmosphere:**
The Spandau Christmas Market has a long history, and its roots can be traced back to the medieval period. The market's location in Spandau's Altstadt adds to its historic charm, with its cobblestone streets, half-timbered houses, and historic churches providing a perfect backdrop for the festivities. The market's atmosphere is warm and welcoming, with a focus on community and tradition. It's a place where locals and visitors alike come together to celebrate the season, making it one of the most authentic Christmas markets in Berlin.

**What to Expect:**

The Spandau Christmas Market is known for its wide variety of stalls, which offer everything from traditional crafts and handmade gifts to local foods and drinks. The market is especially famous for its regional specialties, such as smoked fish, Spandauer Christstollen (a type of Christmas cake), and Berliner Pfannkuchen (a type of jelly-filled doughnut). Many of the vendors are local artisans who take pride in their work, and you'll find a range of unique items that make perfect gifts or souvenirs.

One of the highlights of the Spandau Christmas Market is its medieval section, where visitors can step back in time and experience a traditional Christmas market as it might have been centuries ago. Here, you'll find stalls selling handmade candles, pottery, and leather goods, as well as demonstrations of traditional crafts such as blacksmithing and wood carving. The medieval section also features live entertainment, including performances by minstrels, jugglers, and acrobats, creating a lively and festive atmosphere.

In addition to its shopping and entertainment options, the Spandau Christmas Market offers a range of activities for visitors of all ages. The market's central square features a large Christmas tree and a stage where local choirs and bands perform holiday music. There are also rides and attractions for children, including a carousel and a miniature train that runs through the market. The market's emphasis on tradition and community makes it a great place to experience the true spirit of Christmas in Berlin.

**Practical Tips:**
The Spandau Christmas Market typically runs from late November until just before Christmas, with extended hours on weekends. The market is spread out over several streets and squares, so be prepared to do some walking as you explore. The market is family-friendly, with plenty of activities for children, and there is no entrance fee. Spandau is easily accessible by public transport from central Berlin, making it a convenient destination for a day trip or an evening visit.

Berlin's traditional Christmas markets offer a unique and enchanting way to experience the holiday season. Each market has its own distinct character, from the elegance of the Gendarmenmarkt Christmas Market to the historic charm of the Spandau Christmas Market. Whether you're looking to shop for handmade gifts, indulge in traditional German holiday foods, or simply soak up the festive atmosphere, Berlin's Christmas markets have something for everyone.

As you explore these markets, you'll discover that they are not just places to shop, but vibrant social hubs where people come together to celebrate the season. The combination of history, culture, and festive cheer makes Berlin's Christmas markets a must-visit destination for anyone looking to experience the magic of Christmas in one of Europe's most dynamic cities. So bundle up, grab a cup of Glühwein, and immerse yourself in the warmth and wonder of Berlin at Christmas.

## 1.2 Alternative and Themed Markets

Berlin is renowned for its traditional Christmas markets, but it also offers a diverse array of alternative and themed markets that reflect the city's creative, inclusive, and eclectic spirit. These markets cater to various interests and communities, providing a unique twist on the traditional Christmas market experience. In this section, we will explore three of Berlin's most distinctive alternative markets: The Eco-Friendly Market at Kollwitzplatz, The LGBTQ+ Christmas Avenue at Nollendorfplatz, and The Medieval Market at RAW Gelände. Each of these markets offers a fresh perspective on the holiday season, allowing visitors to experience Berlin's vibrant culture in new and exciting ways.

### The Eco-Friendly Market at Kollwitzplatz

Berlin has long been at the forefront of the environmental movement, and this commitment to sustainability is evident in its Christmas celebrations. The Eco-Friendly Market at Kollwitzplatz is a shining example of how festive traditions can be celebrated in an environmentally conscious way. Located in the heart of Prenzlauer Berg, one of Berlin's trendiest neighborhoods, this market offers visitors the chance to enjoy the holiday season while minimizing their environmental impact.

**History and Atmosphere:**
The Eco-Friendly Market at Kollwitzplatz was established to provide a sustainable alternative to traditional Christmas markets. It reflects Berlin's progressive values and commitment to environmental stewardship. The market is held in the charming Kollwitzplatz, a leafy square surrounded by beautifully restored Altbau (old buildings) that adds to the market's cozy and welcoming atmosphere. The market's layout is designed to minimize waste and energy consumption, with stalls made from recycled materials and energy-efficient lighting throughout.

**What to Expect:**
At the Eco-Friendly Market, you'll find a carefully curated selection of goods that prioritize sustainability, ethical production, and local craftsmanship. Stalls offer a wide range of eco-friendly products, from organic food and drinks to handmade crafts and gifts made from recycled or upcycled materials. You'll find everything from beautifully designed reusable shopping bags to artisanal soaps made from natural ingredients. Many of the vendors are local artisans and small businesses, reflecting Berlin's vibrant maker culture.

Food and drink at the Eco-Friendly Market are also sustainably sourced. You can enjoy organic Glühwein, made with locally produced wine, or indulge in vegan and vegetarian holiday treats that are as delicious as they are ethical. The market also emphasizes reducing food waste, with many vendors offering smaller portions or using surplus ingredients from local farms. There's even a stall dedicated to educating visitors about sustainable living, offering tips and resources on how to reduce your carbon footprint during the holiday season.

Entertainment at the Eco-Friendly Market includes live performances by local musicians, many of whom incorporate themes of environmental awareness into their music. There are also workshops and activities for children that focus on sustainability, such as DIY craft sessions where kids can make their own Christmas ornaments from recycled materials. The market's emphasis on education and community engagement makes it a great destination for families and anyone interested in celebrating Christmas in a more responsible way.

**Practical Tips:**
The Eco-Friendly Market at Kollwitzplatz typically runs from late November until Christmas Eve. It is open during the day and into the evening, making it a perfect destination for a leisurely afternoon or a relaxed evening out. As with all outdoor markets in Berlin, be sure to dress warmly, as temperatures can drop significantly in December. The market is easily accessible by public transport, with several tram and U-Bahn (subway) stations nearby. If you're looking to do some holiday shopping, bring your own reusable bags to carry your

purchases and consider arriving early to avoid the crowds.

## The LGBTQ+ Christmas Avenue at Nollendorfplatz

Berlin has a well-deserved reputation as one of the most LGBTQ+ friendly cities in the world, and this inclusivity extends to its Christmas celebrations. The LGBTQ+ Christmas Avenue at Nollendorfplatz is a vibrant and welcoming market that celebrates diversity and community. Located in the heart of Schöneberg, Berlin's historic gay district, this market is a must-visit for anyone looking to experience the city's festive spirit in an open and inclusive environment.

**History and Atmosphere:**
The LGBTQ+ Christmas Avenue was established as a space where the LGBTQ+ community and its allies could come together to celebrate the holiday season. The market is held at Nollendorfplatz, a historic square that has long been a central gathering place for Berlin's LGBTQ+ community. The market's atmosphere is lively and joyful, with rainbow-colored decorations, inclusive signage, and a warm, welcoming vibe that invites everyone to join in the celebration.

**What to Expect:**
The LGBTQ+ Christmas Avenue offers a unique blend of traditional holiday fare and LGBTQ+ culture. The market's stalls feature a wide range of goods, from rainbow-themed Christmas ornaments and decorations

to handmade crafts and clothing that celebrate LGBTQ+ identity. Many of the vendors are local LGBTQ+ artisans and entrepreneurs, making this market a great place to find one-of-a-kind gifts that support the community.

Food and drink at the LGBTQ+ Christmas Avenue reflect Berlin's diverse culinary scene, with a variety of options to suit all tastes. You can enjoy traditional German Christmas foods, such as Bratwurst and Glühwein, as well as international dishes that reflect the global nature of Berlin's LGBTQ+ community. Vegan and vegetarian options are plentiful, and there are also stalls offering cocktails and other drinks with a festive twist.

One of the highlights of the LGBTQ+ Christmas Avenue is its entertainment program, which includes performances by drag queens, live music from LGBTQ+ artists, and DJ sets that keep the party going well into the night. The market also hosts special events, such as charity fundraisers and community workshops, that make it a hub of activity throughout the holiday season. The inclusive and celebratory atmosphere of the LGBTQ+ Christmas Avenue makes it a unique and unforgettable destination for both locals and visitors.

**Practical Tips:**
The LGBTQ+ Christmas Avenue is open from late November until just before Christmas. It operates in the evenings, making it a perfect destination for a night out during the holiday season. The market is easily accessible by public transport, with Nollendorfplatz

U-Bahn station right next to the market. As with all outdoor events in Berlin, it's important to dress warmly and bring cash, as not all vendors accept credit cards. The market's inclusive atmosphere makes it a great place to visit with friends, family, or as part of a larger group.

## The Medieval Market at RAW Gelände

For a Christmas market experience that transports you back in time, the Medieval Market at RAW Gelände is an absolute must-visit. Located in the trendy Friedrichshain district, this market offers a unique blend of history, culture, and festive fun. Set in the atmospheric surroundings of the RAW Gelände, a former railway maintenance yard turned cultural hub, the Medieval Market immerses visitors in the sights, sounds, and smells of a Christmas long past.

**History and Atmosphere:**
The Medieval Market at RAW Gelände is inspired by the Christmas markets of the Middle Ages, where townspeople would gather to celebrate the holiday season with food, drink, and merriment. The market's location at the RAW Gelände adds to its authenticity, with the historic industrial buildings providing a dramatic backdrop for the festivities. The market is designed to evoke the feel of a medieval village, with stalls made from wood and thatch, torch-lit pathways, and vendors dressed in period costume.

**What to Expect:**
The Medieval Market offers a wide range of goods and experiences that are sure to delight visitors of all ages. Stalls at the market feature handmade crafts and gifts that are inspired by medieval traditions, such as leather goods, hand-forged metalwork, and pottery. You'll also find vendors selling traditional holiday items, such as wreaths and candles, that have been crafted using methods that date back centuries.

Food and drink at the Medieval Market are a highlight of the experience. The market offers a variety of traditional medieval fare, such as roasted meats, hearty stews, and fresh-baked bread. You can wash it all down with a mug of hot mead or mulled wine, served in earthenware cups that add to the authenticity of the experience. There are also plenty of sweet treats on offer, including gingerbread and marzipan, that will satisfy any holiday cravings.

Entertainment at the Medieval Market is truly unique, with performances that transport visitors back to the days of knights and minstrels. The market features live music played on traditional instruments, such as lutes and hurdy-gurdies, as well as performances by fire dancers, jugglers, and acrobats. There are also opportunities for visitors to participate in medieval-themed activities, such as archery, sword fighting, and crafts workshops. The market's immersive atmosphere makes it a magical place to experience the holiday season in a completely different way.

**Practical Tips:**
The Medieval Market at RAW Gelände typically runs from late November until Christmas. It is open in the evenings and on weekends, making it a perfect destination for a weekend outing or an evening of festive fun. The market is located in the heart of Friedrichshain, easily accessible by public transport. As with all outdoor markets in Berlin, be sure to dress warmly and bring cash, as some vendors may not accept credit cards. The market's family-friendly atmosphere makes it a great place to visit with children, who will love the chance to experience a medieval Christmas.

Berlin's alternative and themed Christmas markets offer a refreshing and exciting take on the traditional holiday experience. From the sustainable practices of the Eco-Friendly Market at Kollwitzplatz to the vibrant inclusivity of the LGBTQ+ Christmas Avenue at Nollendorfplatz and the immersive historical experience of the Medieval Market at RAW Gelände, these markets showcase the diversity and creativity that make Berlin one of the world's most dynamic cities. Each market offers a unique way to celebrate the holiday season, reflecting the city's rich cultural heritage and its forward-thinking spirit. Whether you're a local or a visitor, these markets provide an unforgettable way to experience the magic of Christmas in Berlin.

# 1.3 Insider Tips for Navigating the Markets

Exploring Berlin's Christmas markets is a magical experience, but with so many options, it can be overwhelming. To make the most of your visit, it's essential to have some insider knowledge. In this section, we'll provide you with detailed tips on the best times to visit the markets, what festive foods and drinks to try, and the unique souvenirs you should consider taking home. Armed with this information, you'll be well-prepared to enjoy the markets to the fullest and create lasting memories of your holiday trip to Berlin.

## Best Times to Visit

Timing your visit to Berlin's Christmas markets can greatly impact your experience. While the markets are enchanting at any time, there are certain periods and hours that offer distinct advantages depending on what you're looking for.

**Weekdays vs. Weekends:**
Weekends are the busiest times at Berlin's Christmas markets, as locals and tourists alike flock to the stalls. While the lively atmosphere can be enjoyable, it can also mean large crowds and longer lines. If you prefer a more relaxed experience, visiting on a weekday is ideal. Mondays to Thursdays are generally quieter, allowing you to explore the markets at a leisurely pace. This is also a great time to chat with vendors and learn more

about their products, as they have more time to engage with customers.

### Mornings vs. Evenings:

The time of day you choose to visit can also influence your experience. Mornings tend to be less crowded, making them perfect for families with young children or anyone who wants to avoid the hustle and bustle. The markets typically open around 10 or 11 a.m., and the early hours offer a peaceful atmosphere, ideal for browsing the stalls and enjoying a warm drink without the crowds.

Evenings, however, are when the markets truly come to life. As the sun sets and the lights twinkle on, the markets transform into a festive wonderland. The air fills with the scent of roasting chestnuts and mulled wine, and the sound of live music adds to the magical ambiance. If you're looking to soak in the full festive spirit, visiting in the evening is a must. Just be prepared for larger crowds, especially on Fridays and Saturdays.

### Special Events and Performances:

Many of Berlin's Christmas markets feature special events, such as live performances, workshops, and themed nights. Checking the schedule ahead of time can help you plan your visit to coincide with these events. For example, some markets have choir performances, fire shows, or even ice skating rinks that are open only during certain hours. Attending these events can add an extra layer of excitement to your market experience.

**Weather Considerations:**
Berlin in December can be chilly, with temperatures often hovering around freezing. While snow adds to the festive atmosphere, it's important to dress warmly and be prepared for the cold. If possible, check the weather forecast before heading out. Visiting on a clear, crisp day can make for a more enjoyable experience, as you'll be able to explore the markets without worrying about rain or snow.

**Planning Your Route:**
If you're planning to visit multiple markets in one day, it's helpful to plan your route in advance. Berlin's Christmas markets are spread throughout the city, and while public transport is excellent, traveling between markets can take time. Prioritize the markets you're most interested in and group them by location to minimize travel time. For example, you could spend a day exploring the markets in the Mitte district, which include the popular Gendarmenmarkt and Alexanderplatz markets, before heading to Charlottenburg Palace or the eco-friendly market at Kollwitzplatz the next day.

What to Eat and Drink

One of the highlights of visiting Berlin's Christmas markets is indulging in the delicious food and drink on offer. The markets are a feast for the senses, with a wide variety of traditional German treats, international flavors, and seasonal specialties. Knowing what to try is essential to making the most of your culinary experience.

**Traditional German Delicacies:**
Berlin's Christmas markets offer a range of traditional German foods that are perfect for warming up on a cold winter's day. Here are some must-try items:

- **Bratwurst:** A classic German sausage, usually served in a bread roll with mustard or ketchup. It's a simple yet satisfying treat that you'll find at nearly every market.
- **Kartoffelpuffer:** These crispy potato pancakes are a favorite at Christmas markets. They're often served with applesauce or garlic sauce, making them a delicious savory snack.
- **Flammkuchen:** Often referred to as German pizza, Flammkuchen is a thin, crispy flatbread topped with crème fraîche, onions, and bacon. It's a tasty and filling option, perfect for sharing.
- **Lebkuchen:** These spiced gingerbread cookies are a holiday staple in Germany. They come in various shapes and sizes, often decorated with icing and nuts. They make for a sweet treat or a lovely gift to take home.

**Seasonal Beverages:**
No visit to a Christmas market is complete without

sampling the festive drinks on offer. Here are some of the most popular options:

- **Glühwein:** The quintessential Christmas market drink, Glühwein is a hot, spiced wine that warms you from the inside out. It's typically made with red wine, but you'll also find variations made with white wine or even rosé. Look out for stands offering Glühwein in commemorative mugs, which you can take home as a souvenir.

- **Feuerzangenbowle:** A more elaborate version of Glühwein, Feuerzangenbowle involves adding a sugar loaf soaked in rum to the hot wine and then setting it on fire. The resulting drink is both sweet and potent, perfect for warming up on a cold night.

- **Hot Chocolate:** For those who prefer non-alcoholic beverages, hot chocolate is a great choice. Many stalls offer rich, creamy hot chocolate, often topped with whipped cream or marshmallows.

- **Eierpunsch:** A festive egg-based punch similar to eggnog, Eierpunsch is made with eggs, sugar, white wine, and spices, and is served warm. It's a unique and delicious holiday treat that's worth trying.

**International Flavors:**
Berlin's diverse culinary scene is reflected in its Christmas markets, where you'll find a wide range of international foods. Whether you're in the mood for

Spanish churros, French crêpes, or Hungarian lángos, there's something to satisfy every craving. Many markets also feature vegan and vegetarian options, ensuring that everyone can enjoy the festive fare.

**Sweet Treats:**
If you have a sweet tooth, Berlin's Christmas markets won't disappoint. In addition to Lebkuchen, you'll find a variety of other sweet treats, such as:

- **Stollen:** A traditional German Christmas cake, Stollen is a dense, fruit-filled loaf often dusted with powdered sugar. It's rich and flavorful, making it a popular choice during the holiday season.
- **Marzipan:** This almond-based confection is a holiday favorite in Germany. You'll find marzipan in various shapes and flavors, from simple almond logs to intricately shaped fruits and figures.
- **Candied Nuts:** The scent of roasting nuts is a hallmark of Christmas markets. You'll find stands selling candied almonds, hazelnuts, and other nuts coated in a sweet, crunchy glaze.

## Unique Souvenirs to Buy

One of the joys of visiting Berlin's Christmas markets is the opportunity to shop for unique, handcrafted gifts and souvenirs. From traditional crafts to contemporary designs, the markets offer a wide range of items that make for perfect holiday keepsakes or gifts for loved ones.

## Handcrafted Ornaments:

Christmas ornaments are among the most popular items at Berlin's markets. You'll find a stunning array of handmade ornaments, ranging from delicate glass baubles to wooden carvings. Many stalls offer traditional German ornaments, such as nutcrackers and Räuchermännchen (smoking men), as well as more modern designs. These ornaments make for beautiful additions to your Christmas tree and are a lovely way to remember your visit.

## Artisanal Crafts:

Berlin's Christmas markets are a showcase for local artisans, offering a wide range of handcrafted goods. Look out for stalls selling pottery, textiles, and jewelry, all made by skilled craftspeople. These items often have a unique, personal touch that you won't find in mass-produced goods, making them ideal for thoughtful, one-of-a-kind gifts.

## Local Specialties:

If you're looking for souvenirs that reflect Berlin's local culture, there are plenty of options to choose from. For example, you might find Berliner Weisse beer glasses, which are perfect for enjoying the city's famous wheat beer. Another great option is Berlin-themed artwork or photography, capturing the city's iconic landmarks and vibrant street scenes. Many markets also offer locally made food products, such as honey, jams, and mustard, which make for delicious and authentic gifts.

**Christmas Decorations:**
In addition to ornaments, Berlin's markets offer a variety of other Christmas decorations that can add a festive touch to your home. Look for handmade wreaths, candle holders, and table centerpieces that feature natural materials like pinecones, berries, and dried flowers. You'll also find traditional German decorations, such as Advent calendars and pyramids, which are both beautiful and functional.

**Toys and Games:**
For families with children, the Christmas markets are a treasure trove of traditional toys and games. You'll find wooden toys, puzzles, and stuffed animals that are beautifully crafted and built to last. Many of these toys are made using traditional methods and materials, making them a charming and timeless gift for children.

**Books and Stationery:**
Berlin's Christmas markets often feature stalls selling books, journals, and other stationery items. These can make for thoughtful gifts, especially if you find something that reflects your own interests or those of the recipient. Look for books on Berlin's history or culture, as well as beautifully designed notebooks and calendars.

**Supporting Local Artisans:**

One of the best things about shopping at Berlin's Christmas markets is the opportunity to support local artisans and small businesses. By purchasing handmade goods, you're not only taking home a unique souvenir but also contributing to the livellhoods of the people who create them. Many of the vendors at the markets are passionate about their craft and take pride in their work, so you can feel good knowing that your purchase is making a positive impact.

# Chapter 2: Illuminating Berlin: Christmas Lights and Decorations

## 2.1 Iconic Streets and Neighborhoods

Berlin's transformation during the holiday season is nothing short of magical. The city's streets, squares, and neighborhoods come alive with dazzling lights and festive decorations, turning Berlin into a winter wonderland. In this chapter, we'll take you on a journey through the most iconic streets and neighborhoods where the Christmas lights and decorations are at their best. We'll explore Kurfürstendamm, Unter den Linden, and Potsdamer Platz—each offering a unique take on Berlin's holiday spirit.

### Kurfürstendamm: The Grand Boulevard of Lights

**Historical Significance and Holiday Transformation**
Kurfürstendamm, often referred to simply as Ku'damm, is one of Berlin's most famous boulevards. Historically, it has been the center of West Berlin's social and cultural life, lined with luxury boutiques, cafes, and theaters. During the Christmas season, Kurfürstendamm is transformed into a grand spectacle of lights and decorations, making it a must-visit for anyone in the city during the holidays.

The entire length of Ku'damm, stretching from Breitscheidplatz to Halensee, is adorned with thousands of twinkling lights. The trees that line the boulevard are wrapped in strings of lights, creating a tunnel of illumination that is both mesmerizing and enchanting. The grand facades of the buildings, including iconic department stores like KaDeWe, are draped in festive decorations, adding to the street's opulent holiday atmosphere.

**Key Attractions and Highlights**
One of the highlights of Kurfürstendamm during the Christmas season is the Weihnachtsmarkt am Gedächtniskirche, or Christmas Market at the Kaiser Wilhelm Memorial Church. This market is set against the backdrop of the historic church, which is itself beautifully illuminated. The market features a wide array of stalls selling traditional German Christmas goods, from handcrafted ornaments to delicious food and drink. The scent of roasted chestnuts, mulled wine, and gingerbread fills the air, making it a sensory delight.

In addition to the market, Kurfürstendamm is home to some of the best shopping in Berlin. The street's luxury boutiques and department stores go all out with their holiday window displays, which are a spectacle in their own right. These displays are often themed and meticulously designed, drawing crowds who come to admire the creativity and craftsmanship. Whether you're in the mood for some holiday shopping or simply want to soak in the festive atmosphere, Ku'damm offers an unforgettable experience.

**Best Times to Visit and Insider Tips**

To fully appreciate the lights and decorations on Kurfürstendamm, it's best to visit in the early evening, just as the sun sets and the lights begin to twinkle. This is when the boulevard is at its most magical, with the glow of the lights creating a warm and inviting atmosphere. While Ku'damm can get crowded, especially on weekends, the crowds add to the festive spirit, making it a lively and vibrant place to be.

For a more leisurely experience, consider visiting on a weekday when the crowds are thinner. If you're interested in shopping, many of the stores along Ku'damm offer extended holiday hours, allowing you to browse the festive displays at your own pace. And don't forget to bring your camera—Kurfürstendamm is one of the most photogenic spots in Berlin during the holiday season, offering countless opportunities for stunning photos.

## Unter den Linden: The Heart of Berlin's Festive Spirit

**A Historic Avenue with a Festive Flair**

Unter den Linden is Berlin's most famous avenue, steeped in history and lined with some of the city's most important landmarks. Stretching from the Brandenburg Gate to the Museum Island, this grand boulevard is a central part of Berlin's identity. During the Christmas season, Unter den Linden is transformed into a dazzling display of lights and decorations, becoming the heart of Berlin's festive celebrations.

The trees that line Unter den Linden are draped with thousands of fairy lights, creating a canopy of illumination that guides visitors along the avenue. The historic buildings along the boulevard, including the State Opera House and Humboldt University, are adorned with elegant decorations, adding to the avenue's timeless charm. The lights on Unter den Linden are more understated compared to the extravagance of Kurfürstendamm, but they exude a classic beauty that is both sophisticated and enchanting.

**Festive Highlights and Attractions**
One of the key attractions along Unter den Linden during the Christmas season is the annual Christmas market at Bebelplatz. This market is set in the historic square, surrounded by grand buildings like the State Opera House and St. Hedwig's Cathedral. The market itself is a cozy affair, featuring stalls selling traditional crafts, food, and drink. The atmosphere is intimate and relaxed, making it a perfect spot to unwind and enjoy the festive spirit.

Another highlight of Unter den Linden during the holidays is the Brandenburg Gate, one of Berlin's most iconic landmarks. The gate is beautifully illuminated, often with a large Christmas tree standing in front of it. This is a popular spot for visitors to take photos, and the sight of the illuminated gate against the night sky is truly breathtaking. The combination of history and holiday cheer makes Unter den Linden a must-visit during the Christmas season.

### Navigating Unter den Linden: Tips for Visitors

Visiting Unter den Linden during the holidays is a must for anyone looking to experience Berlin's festive spirit. The best time to visit is in the early evening, when the lights are at their most enchanting, and the crowds are just beginning to gather. Walking along the avenue from the Brandenburg Gate to Museum Island is a wonderful way to take in the sights, with plenty of opportunities to stop for a warm drink or snack along the way.

If you're interested in exploring the Christmas market at Bebelplatz, try to visit during the week when the market is less crowded. This will give you more time to browse the stalls and enjoy the festive atmosphere without feeling rushed. And don't forget to take a moment to admire the illuminated landmarks along the way—Unter den Linden is full of historic sites that are particularly beautiful when lit up during the holidays.

## Potsdamer Platz: Modern Festivities in the Heart of Berlin

### A Hub of Holiday Activity

Potsdamer Platz is one of Berlin's most vibrant and modern areas, known for its striking architecture and bustling atmosphere. During the Christmas season, Potsdamer Platz is transformed into a hub of holiday activity, offering a unique blend of traditional and contemporary festivities. This is where Berlin's modern spirit meets holiday cheer, making it a must-visit destination for anyone looking to experience the city's festive side.

The centerpiece of Potsdamer Platz during the holidays is the Winterwelt (Winter World) festival, which takes over the square with a variety of attractions and activities. From ice skating rinks to toboggan runs, Winterwelt offers plenty of fun for visitors of all ages. The square is also adorned with festive lights and decorations, creating a lively and cheerful atmosphere that is perfect for enjoying the holiday season.

**Winterwelt at Potsdamer Platz: A Festive Wonderland**
Winterwelt is one of Berlin's most popular holiday events, drawing locals and tourists alike to Potsdamer Platz. The festival features a large ice skating rink where visitors can glide under the twinkling lights while surrounded by the modern skyscrapers that define the area. Ice skating at Potsdamer Platz is a quintessential Berlin holiday experience, offering a fun and festive way to enjoy the winter season.

Another highlight of Winterwelt is the toboggan run, which is set up in the middle of the square. Visitors can race down the icy slope on sleds, adding a bit of adrenaline to their holiday celebrations. The toboggan run is especially popular with families and children, but it's also a fun activity for anyone looking to embrace the winter spirit.

In addition to the skating and sledding, Winterwelt features a range of stalls selling food, drinks, and holiday goods. You can warm up with a cup of Glühwein, enjoy a bratwurst, or shop for unique gifts and souvenirs. The festival atmosphere at Potsdamer Platz is infectious, making it a great place to spend an afternoon or evening during the holidays.

**Exploring Potsdamer Platz: What to See and Do**
Potsdamer Platz is not just about Winterwelt—there's plenty more to see and do in the area during the holidays. The square is home to some of Berlin's most iconic modern architecture, including the Sony Center and the Deutsche Bahn Tower, both of which are beautifully illuminated during the festive season. The combination of modern buildings and holiday lights creates a stunning visual contrast, making Potsdamer Platz a unique destination for holiday sightseeing.

If you're looking for a bit of culture, the area around Potsdamer Platz is also home to several museums and theaters. The Berlin Philharmonic, one of the world's leading orchestras, often hosts special holiday concerts during the season. Attending a concert is a wonderful way to experience Berlin's rich cultural scene while enjoying the festive atmosphere.

For those interested in shopping, Potsdamer Platz offers a variety of options, from high-end boutiques to popular retail chains. The nearby Mall of Berlin is one of the city's largest shopping centers, and it's beautifully decorated for the holidays. Whether you're looking for last-minute gifts or just want to browse, Potsdamer Platz is a great place to do some holiday shopping.

**Tips for Visiting Potsdamer Platz During the Holidays**

Potsdamer Platz is one of Berlin's busiest areas, especially during the holiday season, so it's important to plan your visit accordingly. If you're interested in ice skating or tobogganing at Winterwelt, try to visit early in the day or on a weekday to avoid the crowds. Weekends can be particularly busy, but the lively atmosphere is part of the charm, so don't let the crowds deter you from visiting.

For a unique perspective on the holiday lights, consider taking a ride on the Panoramapunkt, an observation deck located in the Kollhoff Tower at Potsdamer Platz. The deck offers panoramic views of the city, and during the holidays, you can see the twinkling lights of Berlin from above—a truly magical sight.

## 2.2 Spectacular Light Shows and Installations

Berlin during Christmas is a city transformed by light. The city's architecture and public spaces serve as canvases for spectacular light shows and installations, turning the urban landscape into a glittering wonderland. In this section, we will explore three of the most breathtaking light displays: the Berlin Cathedral Light Display, the Brandenburg Gate Illumination, and the Sony Center Christmas Lights. These installations are not just decorations; they are artistic expressions that celebrate the holiday season in a uniquely Berlin style.

## Berlin Cathedral Light Display: A Symphony of Light and History

### The Iconic Berliner Dom in a New Light

Berlin Cathedral, or Berliner Dom, is one of the city's most significant landmarks, known for its stunning architecture and historical importance. During the Christmas season, this iconic structure is brought to life through a breathtaking light display that highlights its grandeur while adding a festive touch. The Berlin Cathedral Light Display is a must-see for visitors and locals alike, offering a unique way to experience this historic site.

The light display at Berlin Cathedral is a carefully choreographed show that uses advanced projection mapping technology to cover the building's façade with intricate patterns, vibrant colors, and festive imagery. The result is a dynamic visual experience that accentuates the cathedral's architectural features, such as its domes, columns, and ornate carvings. The light show is often accompanied by music, creating a multisensory experience that leaves a lasting impression on all who witness it.

## The Themes and Messages Behind the Display
Each year, the light display at Berlin Cathedral takes on a different theme, often reflecting aspects of Berlin's culture, history, or the broader Christmas message. Past displays have included themes like "Peace on Earth," showcasing doves and olive branches, and "Unity and Diversity," featuring a mosaic of cultural symbols and colors. These themes are not only visually stunning but also thought-provoking, inviting viewers to reflect on the deeper meanings of the holiday season.

The use of light at Berlin Cathedral goes beyond mere decoration. It serves as a medium for storytelling, conveying messages of hope, peace, and unity that resonate with the spirit of Christmas. The interplay of light and shadow, combined with the historical backdrop of the cathedral, creates a powerful narrative that is both visually captivating and emotionally moving.

## When and How to Experience the Light Show
The Berlin Cathedral Light Display typically runs from late November through the end of December, with shows taking place several times each evening. To fully appreciate the display, it's best to arrive early to secure a good viewing spot, as the area around the cathedral can become quite crowded. The display is best viewed from the Lustgarten, the large park in front of the

cathedral, where you can take in the full scale of the light show.

For those interested in capturing the light display on camera, tripods are allowed in the park, making it easier to take long-exposure shots that capture the intricate details of the projection. The display is also an excellent opportunity for a romantic evening stroll or a family outing, as the festive atmosphere around the cathedral is filled with holiday cheer.

## Brandenburg Gate Illumination: A Symbol of Berlin Shines Bright

### A Historic Monument Illuminated

The Brandenburg Gate is arguably Berlin's most recognizable landmark, symbolizing the city's history and resilience. During the Christmas season, this historic monument becomes the centerpiece of one of Berlin's most spectacular light displays. The Brandenburg Gate Illumination is a celebration of light that highlights the gate's architectural beauty while adding a festive glow to the heart of the city.

The illumination of the Brandenburg Gate is a simple yet powerful display that emphasizes the monument's neoclassical design. The gate's columns and archways are bathed in soft, warm light, creating a serene and majestic atmosphere. The illumination often includes subtle color changes that enhance the visual impact, making the gate appear even more grand and imposing against the night sky.

## The Cultural and Symbolic Significance
The Brandenburg Gate is more than just a beautiful monument; it is a symbol of Berlin's history, particularly its role in the reunification of Germany. The decision to illuminate the gate during the holiday season reflects its significance as a symbol of hope, peace, and unity—values that are central to the Christmas spirit. The light display at the Brandenburg Gate serves as a reminder of the city's journey through history and its ongoing commitment to these ideals.

During the holiday season, the Brandenburg Gate becomes a gathering place for Berliners and visitors, who come to admire the lights and reflect on the monument's significance. The atmosphere around the gate is festive yet contemplative, offering a moment of peace and reflection amidst the hustle and bustle of the holiday season. The illumination also serves as a backdrop for various events, including Christmas concerts and public gatherings, further enhancing its role as a symbol of unity and celebration.

## Planning Your Visit to the Brandenburg Gate
The Brandenburg Gate is located in Pariser Platz, a central and easily accessible part of Berlin. The best time to visit is in the early evening, just as the lights are turned on and the crowds begin to gather. The gate is beautifully illuminated from all sides, but the view from

the west, looking towards the Tiergarten, is particularly striking.

If you're interested in photography, the Brandenburg Gate offers excellent opportunities for capturing stunning night shots. The wide-open space of Pariser Platz allows for creative compositions, whether you're photographing the gate on its own or including the festive decorations that often surround it. A wide-angle lens is recommended to capture the full scope of the illumination, and a tripod will help with long-exposure shots.

## Sony Center Christmas Lights: A Modern Light Spectacle

### A Futuristic Holiday Experience

The Sony Center at Potsdamer Platz is one of Berlin's most modern architectural marvels, known for its striking design and innovative use of space. During the Christmas season, the Sony Center is transformed into a futuristic wonderland, with an elaborate light display that combines cutting-edge technology with holiday cheer. The Sony Center Christmas Lights are a must-see for anyone looking to experience a different side of Berlin's holiday celebrations.

The centerpiece of the Sony Center's Christmas display is its massive, tent-like roof, which is illuminated with thousands of LED lights. These lights change color and pattern, creating a dynamic, ever-changing spectacle that is both mesmerizing and festive. The effect is heightened by the surrounding glass and steel structures, which reflect the lights and add to the sense of being in a futuristic environment.

**The Unique Atmosphere of the Sony Center**
What sets the Sony Center apart from other holiday light displays in Berlin is its unique atmosphere. The combination of modern architecture, high-tech lighting, and festive decorations creates an experience that feels both contemporary and magical. The light display at the Sony Center is synchronized with music, adding to the immersive experience and making it feel like you've stepped into a holiday movie set.

The Sony Center is also home to a variety of shops, restaurants, and entertainment venues, making it a great place to spend an evening during the holiday season. You can enjoy a meal at one of the many restaurants while taking in the light show, or do some holiday shopping at the center's boutiques. The atmosphere is lively and upbeat, making it a perfect destination for families, couples, and groups of friends.

**Tips for Enjoying the Sony Center Christmas Lights**
The Sony Center is located at Potsdamer Platz, one of Berlin's busiest and most accessible areas. The light display runs throughout the holiday season, with the best time to visit being in the early evening when the lights are at their most vibrant. The center's modern design means that you can enjoy the display from a

variety of angles, so take some time to explore the space and find the perfect spot to admire the lights.

For photographers, the Sony Center offers a unique challenge. The combination of bright lights, reflective surfaces, and moving patterns can be tricky to capture, but the results can be stunning. A tripod is essential for steady shots, and a fast lens will help you capture the vibrant colors of the display. Experiment with different angles and compositions to make the most of the futuristic setting.

# 2.3 Photography Tips for Capturing the Magic

Berlin's Christmas lights and decorations offer countless opportunities for stunning photography. Whether you're using a professional camera or just your smartphone, capturing the magic of Berlin during the holidays requires a bit of skill and creativity. In this section, we'll provide you with tips and tricks to help you take beautiful photos of Berlin's light displays, from the best spots for night photography to editing techniques that will make your images shine.

## Best Spots for Night Photography

### Choosing the Perfect Location
Berlin is full of picturesque spots where you can capture the city's holiday lights in all their glory. Some of the best locations for night photography include

Kurfürstendamm, Unter den Linden, Potsdamer Platz, and, of course, the iconic landmarks like the Brandenburg Gate and Berlin Cathedral. Each of these locations offers its own unique perspective on the city's festive decorations, so it's worth exploring multiple spots to get a variety of shots.

Kurfürstendamm is ideal for capturing the bustling holiday atmosphere, with its grand boulevard lined with twinkling lights and decorated shop windows. Unter den Linden, with its historic buildings and elegant light displays, offers a more classic and serene setting. Potsdamer Platz provides a modern contrast, with its futuristic architecture and vibrant light shows. And for those iconic Berlin shots, the Brandenburg Gate and Berlin Cathedral are must-visit locations.

**Timing Your Shots**
The best time to capture Berlin's holiday lights is during the blue hour, the period just after sunset when the sky is still tinged with blue, but the city lights are beginning to shine. This time of day offers a beautiful contrast between the natural light and the artificial illumination, making your photos more dynamic and visually interesting.

Another great time to shoot is late at night when the crowds have thinned out, and you can capture the lights in a more peaceful and undisturbed setting. This is particularly useful if you want to focus on the details of the light displays or create more artistic compositions.

## Maximizing Your Smartphone's Capabilities

Smartphone cameras have come a long way in recent years, and with the right techniques, you can capture stunning photos of Berlin's Christmas lights using just your phone. Start by familiarizing yourself with your phone's camera settings. Most smartphones have a night mode or low-light setting that can help you take clearer, more detailed photos in low light conditions. Use this mode to reduce noise and improve the quality of your night shots.

When photographing lights, it's important to keep your phone steady to avoid blurry images. If you don't have a tripod, try resting your phone on a stable surface or using a nearby object to support it. You can also use the timer function to reduce camera shake caused by pressing the shutter button.

## Composing Your Shots

Composition is key to creating visually appealing photos, whether you're using a smartphone or a professional camera. When photographing Berlin's Christmas lights, look for interesting angles and perspectives that highlight the beauty of the displays. For example, you can use leading lines, such as the illuminated trees along Unter den Linden, to draw the viewer's eye into the frame. Reflections, whether in shop windows or puddles on the ground, can also add depth and interest to your photos.

Experiment with different compositions, such as framing the Brandenburg Gate through the arches of a nearby building or capturing the Berlin Cathedral reflected in the Lustgarten's water features. The key is to be creative and think outside the box to create unique and memorable images.

## Editing Tips for the Perfect Holiday Photos

### Enhancing Your Images

Once you've captured your photos, the next step is to edit them to enhance their beauty and make them truly stand out. Whether you're using a smartphone app or professional editing software, there are a few key adjustments you can make to improve your holiday photos.

Start by adjusting the exposure and brightness to bring out the details in the lights. Be careful not to overexpose the highlights, as this can cause the lights to lose their definition. You can also increase the contrast to make the lights pop against the darker areas of the image.

### Playing with Color and Filters

The color of the lights is one of the most striking aspects of Berlin's Christmas displays, so be sure to enhance these colors in your editing process. Adjust the saturation and vibrance to make the colors more vivid, but avoid overdoing it, as this can make the image look unnatural. If the colors of the lights are too warm or cool, use the white balance tool to correct them and achieve a more balanced look.

Filters can also add a festive touch to your photos, but use them sparingly. A subtle filter can enhance the mood of your image without overpowering it. For example, a soft vignette can draw attention to the center of the image, while a slight warmth filter can enhance the cozy holiday feel.

**Final Touches**

Before you finish editing, take a moment to crop and straighten your image if necessary. Removing distractions from the edges of the frame can help focus the viewer's attention on the main subject. Finally, consider adding a touch of sharpening to bring out the details in the lights and make your image crisp and clear.

With these tips, you'll be able to capture the magic of Berlin's Christmas lights and create stunning holiday photos that you'll cherish for years to come. Whether you're a seasoned photographer or just starting out, Berlin's festive displays offer endless opportunities for beautiful and memorable images.

# Chapter 3: Must-See Winter Attractions in Berlin

## 3.1 Historical Sites with a Holiday Twist

Berlin, a city steeped in history, transforms into a winter wonderland during the holiday season. While the city's rich past can be explored year-round, visiting these historical sites in winter offers a unique experience as they take on a festive atmosphere. This chapter explores three must-see historical attractions in Berlin that embrace the holiday spirit, offering visitors a blend of history, culture, and seasonal charm: the Berlin Wall Memorial, the Reichstag Building, and Checkpoint Charlie Museum.

**Berlin Wall Memorial with Winter Exhibits: Reflecting on History Amidst Winter's Quietude**

**A Silent Tribute to the Past**

The Berlin Wall Memorial, located along Bernauer Strasse, stands as a poignant reminder of the city's division during the Cold War. This site is one of Berlin's most significant historical landmarks, offering a deep and reflective experience for visitors who want to understand the impact of the Berlin Wall on the city's history and its people. During the winter months, the Memorial takes on a serene, almost haunting atmosphere, as the snow blankets the ground and muffles the sounds of the bustling city.

The Berlin Wall Memorial stretches for 1.4 kilometers and includes the last piece of the Berlin Wall with the preserved grounds behind it, where the border strip can still be seen. This section of the Wall, along with the Chapel of Reconciliation and the various information stations, tells the story of the Wall's construction, the lives it divided, and its eventual fall in 1989. Winter is a particularly poignant time to visit, as the cold and quiet add to the solemnity of the site, allowing visitors to reflect on the Wall's history in a more personal and contemplative way.

**Winter Exhibits and Special Programs**
During the holiday season, the Berlin Wall Memorial often hosts special winter exhibits that highlight lesser-known aspects of the Wall's history, such as stories of families divided during Christmas or the struggles of East Berliners during the harsh winters of the Cold War. These exhibits, often featuring personal testimonies, photographs, and artifacts, provide a deeper understanding of the human side of the Berlin Wall, making a visit during the winter months particularly meaningful.

In addition to the exhibits, the Memorial also offers guided tours tailored to the winter season. These tours take advantage of the early sunset, using the fading daylight to create a dramatic backdrop for the stories of courage and resilience that are central to the Wall's history. Visitors are encouraged to bundle up and walk through the memorial at dusk, when the lighting creates a powerful and somber atmosphere, perfect for reflecting on the significance of the site.

**The Chapel of Reconciliation: A Beacon of Hope**

At the heart of the Berlin Wall Memorial stands the Chapel of Reconciliation, a simple yet powerful symbol of hope and healing. The original chapel, which stood on this site, was destroyed by East German authorities in 1985. The current chapel, built after the reunification of Germany, is a modern structure made of clay and wood, symbolizing reconciliation and new beginnings. During the winter, the chapel hosts special services and events, including Christmas concerts and candlelit vigils, which add to the sense of reflection and peace that permeates the site.

The Chapel of Reconciliation is also a place for personal reflection. Visitors are welcome to light candles and spend time in quiet contemplation, making it a poignant stop during a winter visit to the Memorial. The chapel's simplicity and warmth provide a stark contrast to the cold and barren landscape of the Wall, offering a space for visitors to connect with the deeper themes of forgiveness and unity that are central to the site's message.

**Reichstag Building and its Winter Gardens: Politics Meets Festive Splendor**

**A Symbol of German Democracy**

The Reichstag Building, home to the German Bundestag (Parliament), is one of Berlin's most iconic landmarks. Known for its historical significance and its striking glass dome, the Reichstag is a must-see for anyone visiting Berlin. During the winter season, the building and its surrounding gardens take on a festive atmosphere, offering visitors a unique way to experience this symbol of German democracy.

The Reichstag's history is deeply intertwined with the story of Berlin itself. Originally completed in 1894, the building was heavily damaged during World War II and later restored in the 1990s after German reunification. Today, the Reichstag stands as a symbol of the country's commitment to democracy and transparency, with the glass dome representing the openness of the German government to its people. During the winter months, the Reichstag is adorned with festive lights and decorations, making it an even more impressive sight against the winter skyline.

**Winter Gardens and Festive Displays**
One of the highlights of visiting the Reichstag in winter is exploring the winter gardens located on the building's rooftop terrace. These gardens, normally lush with greenery during the warmer months, are transformed into a winter wonderland, complete with snow-covered trees, twinkling lights, and festive decorations. The rooftop terrace offers stunning views of Berlin's cityscape, including the Brandenburg Gate, the Berlin Cathedral, and the distant TV Tower, all illuminated for the holiday season.

The Reichstag also hosts special holiday events, including Christmas markets and seasonal exhibitions that explore the building's history and its role in modern Germany. These events are designed to engage visitors of all ages, offering a mix of education, entertainment, and festive cheer. During the Advent season, the Reichstag's dome is often lit up with a special display, creating a beacon of light that can be seen from across the city.

**Visiting the Dome: A Unique Perspective on Berlin**
The Reichstag's glass dome is one of the most popular attractions in Berlin, offering visitors a 360-degree view of the city from a height of 47 meters. The dome, designed by British architect Sir Norman Foster, is a marvel of modern engineering and symbolizes the transparency of Germany's democratic process. Visitors can walk up the spiraling ramp inside the dome to the observation deck at the top, where they can enjoy panoramic views of Berlin's winter landscape.

During the holiday season, visiting the dome is a particularly special experience. The city's Christmas lights and decorations can be seen twinkling below, creating a magical scene that is sure to leave a lasting impression. The dome is open to the public year-round, but during the winter months, it's advisable to book a time slot in advance, as the demand is high, especially around the holidays. Guided tours are also available, offering insights into the building's architecture, history, and the significance of the dome itself.

## Checkpoint Charlie Museum's Special Christmas Display: A Cold War Christmas

### A Glimpse into Berlin's Divided Past

Checkpoint Charlie, the most famous border crossing point between East and West Berlin during the Cold War, is another must-see historical site in Berlin. Today, the Checkpoint Charlie Museum, located just steps from the original checkpoint, offers a deep dive into the history of the Berlin Wall and the dramatic escapes that took place at this very spot. During the holiday season, the museum adds a festive touch with a special Christmas display that offers a unique perspective on the Cold War era.

The museum's exhibits focus on the stories of those who attempted to escape from East to West Berlin, often using ingenious and daring methods. These stories are brought to life through photographs, documents, and personal artifacts, making the museum a compelling and emotional experience. In winter, the museum's atmosphere takes on an added layer of poignancy, as visitors are reminded of the hardships faced by Berliners during the cold, dark winters of the Cold War.

### The Christmas Display: A Touch of Festive Nostalgia

The Checkpoint Charlie Museum's special Christmas display is a unique exhibit that blends history with holiday nostalgia. The display features a collection of artifacts and photographs that tell the story of Christmas in divided Berlin, focusing on how the holiday was celebrated on both sides of the Wall. Visitors can see examples of East German Christmas decorations, traditional holiday foods, and even toys that were popular during the era.

One of the highlights of the display is a section dedicated to the "Christmas truce" moments when East and West Berliners would come together, even briefly, to celebrate the holiday season. These moments of unity, whether through shared Christmas carols across the Wall or the exchange of small gifts, offer a heartwarming glimpse into the human spirit that persisted despite the city's division. The museum's Christmas display is a powerful reminder of the resilience and hope that characterized life in Berlin during the Cold War.

**Interactive Exhibits and Seasonal Events**
In addition to the Christmas display, the Checkpoint Charlie Museum offers a range of interactive exhibits that allow visitors to engage more deeply with the history of the Berlin Wall. During the holiday season, the museum also hosts special events, including lectures, film screenings, and workshops that explore the intersection of history and the holiday season. These events provide a deeper understanding of the Cold War era while also offering a festive atmosphere that makes learning about this period of history more accessible and engaging.

The museum's location in the heart of Berlin makes it easy to include in a day of sightseeing. After exploring the museum, visitors can take a short walk to nearby attractions, such as the Topography of Terror or the Jewish Museum, both of which offer additional insights into Berlin's complex history.

## 3.2 Family-Friendly Attractions

Berlin is a city that welcomes families with open arms, and during the Christmas season, it transforms into a magical wonderland that offers plenty of activities for visitors of all ages. Whether you're traveling with young children, teenagers, or a multigenerational group, Berlin has something to delight everyone. From mesmerizing light displays at the zoo to expansive outdoor winter activities and the thrill of ice skating in the heart of the city, these family-friendly attractions provide unforgettable holiday experiences.

**Berlin Zoo's Christmas Lights Safari: A Wild Winter Wonderland**

**A Festive Adventure in the Animal Kingdom**
Berlin Zoo, one of the oldest and most famous zoos in the world, becomes even more enchanting during the Christmas season with its annual Christmas Lights Safari. This event transforms the zoo into a glowing wonderland, where the beauty of nature meets the magic of holiday lights. Families are invited to embark on a nocturnal adventure through the zoo, where they can experience the animal kingdom in a whole new light—literally.

The Christmas Lights Safari features thousands of twinkling lights that illuminate the zoo's pathways, trees, and animal enclosures. The zoo's famous residents, from elephants to penguins, can be seen enjoying their winter surroundings, while light installations create whimsical scenes that captivate the imagination of visitors young and old. The safari is designed to be a self-guided tour, allowing families to explore at their own pace and spend as much time as they like at each exhibit.

## Interactive Displays and Educational Fun

In addition to the light displays, the Christmas Lights Safari offers a range of interactive exhibits that combine fun with education. Children can learn about the animals' winter behaviors, how they adapt to the cold, and the role conservation plays in protecting these species. The zoo often includes special holiday-themed educational activities, such as crafting workshops where kids can create their own animal-themed Christmas ornaments to take home.

For families with younger children, the zoo's playgrounds are also open during the event, providing a perfect spot for little ones to burn off some energy while parents enjoy the festive atmosphere. And of course, no visit to the zoo would be complete without stopping by the petting zoo, where children can get up close and personal with friendly goats, sheep, and other animals.

## Seasonal Treats and Souvenirs

As you wander through the zoo, the aroma of seasonal treats like roasted chestnuts, gingerbread, and mulled wine fills the air. Several food stalls are set up throughout the zoo, offering a variety of holiday snacks and beverages. Warm up with a cup of hot chocolate or indulge in a traditional German bratwurst as you take in the festive surroundings.

Before leaving, be sure to stop by the zoo's gift shop, where you'll find a selection of Christmas-themed souvenirs, from plush animals wearing Santa hats to beautifully crafted ornaments featuring some of the zoo's most beloved animals. These souvenirs make perfect keepsakes to remember your family's magical night at the Berlin Zoo.

### Winter Wonderland at Tempelhofer Feld: A Festive Playground for All Ages

### A Unique Winter Experience on Berlin's Historic Airfield

Tempelhofer Feld, once a bustling airport and now one of Berlin's largest public parks, offers a unique winter experience that combines outdoor recreation with festive fun. During the holiday season, the vast expanse of Tempelhofer Feld is transformed into a Winter Wonderland, where families can enjoy a wide range of activities, from sledding and snowman-building to holiday markets and seasonal performances.

One of the highlights of Winter Wonderland at Tempelhofer Feld is its open-air ice rink, where visitors can glide across the ice while enjoying views of Berlin's skyline. The rink is open to skaters of all skill levels, with special areas designated for beginners and children. Skating lessons are also available for those who want to learn or improve their skills. For those who prefer to stay off the ice, there are plenty of other activities to enjoy, including horse-drawn carriage rides, which offer a charming way to explore the park's winter landscape.

**Family-Friendly Entertainment and Activities**
Winter Wonderland at Tempelhofer Feld is designed with families in mind, offering a variety of entertainment options that cater to all ages. Children will love the festive carousel, where they can take a spin on beautifully decorated horses, while older kids and adults might enjoy trying their hand at curling, a popular winter sport that's easy to learn and fun for all.

The park also hosts a series of live performances throughout the holiday season, including puppet shows, Christmas-themed theater productions, and concerts featuring local musicians and choirs. These performances are often held in heated tents, providing a cozy environment for families to enjoy some culture and entertainment together.

**Exploring the Holiday Market**
In addition to the outdoor activities, Tempelhofer Feld's Winter Wonderland features a charming holiday market,

where visitors can browse stalls selling handcrafted gifts, festive decorations, and seasonal treats. The market is a great place to pick up unique souvenirs, such as hand-knitted scarves, wooden toys, and artisan chocolates. Kids will love visiting the market's Santa Claus, who makes regular appearances to listen to Christmas wishes and pose for photos.

For those looking to indulge in some holiday treats, the market offers a wide selection of food and beverages. Warm up with a cup of Glühwein (mulled wine) or Kinderpunsch (a non-alcoholic version for children), and enjoy a plate of freshly made waffles or a traditional German pretzel. The market's festive atmosphere, combined with the stunning backdrop of Tempelhofer Feld's open spaces, makes it a must-visit destination for families during the holiday season.

**Ice Skating at Alexanderplatz: Gliding in the Heart of the City**

**A Classic Winter Activity in a Historic Setting**
Alexanderplatz, one of Berlin's most famous squares, is a hub of activity during the holiday season, and its ice rink is one of the most popular attractions for families. Located in the heart of the city, the Alexanderplatz ice rink offers visitors the chance to experience the joy of ice skating surrounded by the historic buildings and festive decorations of this iconic location.

The rink is open daily throughout the holiday season and is suitable for skaters of all ages and skill levels. Whether you're an experienced skater looking to show off your moves or a beginner just trying to stay on your feet, the Alexanderplatz ice rink provides a fun and festive environment for all. Skate rentals are available on-site, making it easy for visitors to join in the fun without having to bring their own equipment.

**Festive Ambiance and Nearby Attractions**
What makes ice skating at Alexanderplatz truly special is the festive ambiance that surrounds the rink. The square is adorned with Christmas lights and decorations, creating a magical atmosphere that's perfect for a day or evening of skating. The nearby Berlin TV Tower, one of the city's most recognizable landmarks, adds to the charm, especially when illuminated against the night sky.

After skating, families can explore the surrounding area, which is home to several other holiday attractions, including the Alexanderplatz Christmas Market. This market is one of the largest in Berlin, offering a wide range of stalls selling everything from traditional German crafts to international gifts. The market also features a Ferris wheel, providing stunning views of the city and the chance to see Berlin's holiday lights from above.

For those looking to warm up after a session on the ice, there are plenty of cafés and restaurants nearby where you can enjoy a hot drink or a hearty meal. Whether you're in the mood for a traditional German sausage, a sweet pastry, or something more substantial, Alexanderplatz offers a variety of dining options to suit every taste.

**Special Events and Themed Nights**
Throughout the holiday season, the Alexanderplatz ice rink hosts a series of special events and themed nights that add to the excitement. These events include everything from DJ nights, where you can skate to the latest tunes, to family-friendly afternoons with live music and entertainment for kids. Themed nights often feature costumed characters, light shows, and other surprises that make the skating experience even more memorable.

For families visiting Berlin during the Christmas season, a trip to the Alexanderplatz ice rink is a must. The combination of a central location, festive decorations, and the joy of skating in one of the city's most historic squares makes this a quintessential holiday experience.

# 3.3 Cultural Highlights and Seasonal Performances
Berlin's vibrant cultural scene is one of its most defining features, and during the Christmas season, the city's theaters, concert halls, and cinemas come alive with a range of special performances and events. From classical music concerts at world-renowned venues to enchanting ballet performances and holiday-themed film screenings, Berlin offers a wealth of cultural experiences

that are sure to add a touch of magic to your holiday visit.

### Christmas Concerts at Berlin Philharmonic: A Symphony of Holiday Cheer

#### A World-Class Venue for Classical Music

The Berlin Philharmonic, one of the most prestigious orchestras in the world, is a cultural gem that draws music lovers from around the globe. During the Christmas season, the Philharmonic's concert hall hosts a series of special holiday performances that showcase the talents of its world-class musicians while celebrating the festive spirit.

The Christmas concerts at the Berlin Philharmonic typically feature a mix of classical masterpieces, traditional Christmas carols, and contemporary works that capture the essence of the season. These performances are often conducted by renowned maestros and feature guest soloists who bring their own unique interpretations to the music. The result is a series of concerts that are both uplifting and deeply moving, making them a highlight of Berlin's holiday cultural calendar.

#### A Festive Atmosphere in a Stunning Setting

Attending a concert at the Berlin Philharmonic during the Christmas season is a truly special experience. The concert hall itself is an architectural marvel, with its distinctive tent-like shape and exceptional acoustics that ensure every note resonates with clarity. During the holidays, the hall is decorated with festive touches, adding to the warmth and joy of the season.

For families visiting Berlin, attending a Christmas concert at the Philharmonic is an opportunity to introduce children to the world of classical music in a setting that is both welcoming and awe-inspiring. The orchestra often includes pieces that are familiar to younger audiences, making the experience enjoyable for all ages.

## Nutcracker Ballet at Deutsche Oper: A Timeless Holiday Classic

### A Beloved Holiday Tradition
The Nutcracker ballet is a holiday tradition that has captivated audiences for generations, and at the Deutsche Oper, it is performed with a level of artistry and grace that makes it a must-see event during the Christmas season. This classic ballet, with its enchanting story, beautiful choreography, and Tchaikovsky's iconic score, is brought to life by the talented dancers of the Deutsche Oper's ballet company.

The production at Deutsche Oper is known for its lavish sets, exquisite costumes, and magical stage effects that transport audiences to a world of fantasy and wonder. From the festive Christmas Eve party in the first act to the breathtaking journey through the Land of Sweets, the Nutcracker ballet offers a visual and auditory feast that delights both children and adults alike.

**An Experience to Remember**

Attending the Nutcracker ballet at Deutsche Oper is more than just a cultural outing; it is an experience that creates lasting memories. The joy and excitement on the faces of children as they watch Clara's adventures with the Nutcracker Prince and the battle with the Mouse King is a sight to behold, and for many families, this performance becomes a cherished holiday tradition.

For those visiting Berlin during the Christmas season, securing tickets to the Nutcracker ballet is highly recommended, as performances often sell out well in advance. Whether you're a ballet enthusiast or simply looking to add a touch of magic to your holiday trip, the Nutcracker at Deutsche Oper is an experience not to be missed.

**Holiday Film Screenings at Kino International: A Festive Cinematic Experience**

**A Berlin Cinema with a Rich History**

Kino International, located in the heart of Berlin, is a cinema with a storied past and a reputation for hosting some of the city's most anticipated film screenings. During the Christmas season, Kino International offers a special program of holiday-themed films that provide a cozy and nostalgic way to enjoy the festive season.

The cinema's holiday film series typically includes a mix of classic Christmas movies, family favorites, and new releases that capture the spirit of the season. From heartwarming tales of love and generosity to hilarious comedies that bring joy to audiences of all ages, the films shown at Kino International are carefully curated to appeal to a wide range of tastes.

## A Festive Atmosphere and Special Events

Attending a holiday film screening at Kino International is more than just a trip to the movies; it's an opportunity to immerse yourself in the festive atmosphere of a Berlin Christmas. The cinema is beautifully decorated with holiday lights and ornaments, creating a warm and inviting environment that enhances the movie-going experience.

In addition to regular film screenings, Kino International often hosts special events during the holiday season, such as themed movie nights, sing-alongs, and Q&A sessions with filmmakers and actors. These events add an extra layer of excitement to the holiday film program and provide unique opportunities for movie lovers to engage with the films in new and interactive ways.

For families, a visit to Kino International during the Christmas season is a chance to relax and enjoy some quality time together while watching films that celebrate the magic of the holidays. With its rich history, festive ambiance, and carefully selected film lineup, Kino International offers a cinematic experience that is both entertaining and memorable.

# Chapter 4: Savoring the Flavors of Berlin at Christmas

Berlin's Christmas culinary scene is a feast for the senses, combining traditional German fare with international influences that reflect the city's cosmopolitan spirit. Whether you're indulging in hearty street food at a Christmas market, enjoying a festive meal at a cozy café, or exploring the diverse international cuisines that Berlin has to offer, there's something to satisfy every palate. This chapter takes you on a gastronomic journey through Berlin's Christmas delights, from traditional German dishes to global holiday favorites, and highlights the best places to enjoy a warm, festive meal.

## 4.1 Traditional German Christmas Dishes

Berlin's Christmas season is synonymous with traditional German cuisine, where comfort food takes center stage. The city's Christmas markets, restaurants, and street vendors offer a variety of dishes that are steeped in history and flavor, making them a must-try for any visitor.

### Bratwurst and Glühwein: A Perfect Pair

### The Quintessential German Experience
No visit to a Berlin Christmas market is complete without sampling a grilled bratwurst paired with a steaming mug

of Glühwein (mulled wine). This classic combination is the epitome of German street food, offering a simple yet satisfying meal that warms you from the inside out on a cold winter's day.

Bratwurst, a type of German sausage made from pork, beef, or veal, is often served in a bun with mustard or ketchup. The sausages are grilled to perfection, with a crispy exterior and juicy interior that bursts with flavor. Whether you prefer a classic Thüringer bratwurst or a spicier variation, this savory treat is a staple at Berlin's Christmas markets.

Glühwein, on the other hand, is a traditional hot wine infused with spices like cinnamon, cloves, and star anise, often sweetened with sugar and sometimes enhanced with a splash of brandy or rum. It's the perfect beverage to sip as you stroll through the markets, its warmth providing a welcome reprieve from the chilly air. Some markets also offer variations like white Glühwein or non-alcoholic Kinderpunsch for younger visitors or those who prefer an alcohol-free option.

**Where to Find the Best Bratwurst and Glühwein**
While you can find bratwurst and Glühwein at nearly every Christmas market in Berlin, some locations stand out for their quality and atmosphere. The Gendarmenmarkt Christmas Market, for instance, is renowned for its gourmet food stalls, where you can enjoy a premium bratwurst alongside a glass of artisanal Glühwein. The Charlottenburg Palace Market, with its

historical backdrop, offers a picturesque setting to savor these traditional treats.

For a more rustic experience, head to the Spandau Christmas Market, one of Berlin's oldest and largest markets. Here, you'll find a wide variety of bratwurst options, from classic recipes to regional specialties, all prepared over an open flame for an authentic taste.

**Lebkuchen and Stollen: Sweet Treats**

**A Taste of German Christmas Tradition**
Lebkuchen and Stollen are two iconic German Christmas sweets that have been enjoyed for centuries. These confections are deeply rooted in German culture and are a must-try for anyone visiting Berlin during the holiday season.

Lebkuchen, often referred to as German gingerbread, is a spiced cookie that comes in various shapes and sizes, often decorated with icing or chocolate. The flavors of honey, cinnamon, cloves, and nuts create a rich, aromatic treat that embodies the essence of Christmas. In Berlin, you'll find lebkuchen hearts hanging at market stalls, adorned with festive messages and decorations, making them both a delicious snack and a charming souvenir.

Stollen, a dense fruitcake dusted with powdered sugar, is another traditional Christmas delicacy. Originating in the city of Dresden, stollen is made with a rich dough filled with dried fruits, nuts, and marzipan. Its distinctive flavor and texture have made it a holiday favorite not only in Germany but around the world. Berlin bakeries often offer their own variations of stollen, each with unique touches that reflect the local culinary traditions.

**Where to Find the Best Lebkuchen and Stollen**
To sample the finest lebkuchen and stollen in Berlin, a visit to one of the city's artisanal bakeries is a must. Bäckerei Siebert, one of Berlin's oldest bakeries, is known for its traditional stollen, made using recipes passed down through generations. Their attention to detail and quality ingredients ensure a truly authentic experience.

For lebkuchen, head to the WeihnachtsZauber at Gendarmenmarkt, where you'll find a wide selection of these spiced cookies, often packaged in decorative tins that make for perfect gifts. Many of the market's stalls offer freshly baked lebkuchen, allowing you to enjoy the full depth of flavor that only comes from a freshly made treat.

**Hearty Winter Soups and Stews**

**Comfort Food for Cold Days**
Berlin's winter weather calls for hearty, warming dishes, and nothing fits the bill better than traditional German soups and stews. These dishes are designed to be filling and flavorful, providing both comfort and nourishment during the colder months.

One of the most popular winter soups is **Kartoffelsuppe** (potato soup), a thick and creamy dish made with potatoes, leeks, carrots, and often topped with crispy bacon or sausage. It's a staple in German households and a common offering at Christmas markets, where it's served in large bowls with a side of crusty bread.

Another favorite is **Grünkohl mit Pinkel**, a hearty kale stew that's particularly popular in northern Germany. This dish combines chopped kale with sausages, bacon, and oats, resulting in a robust, flavorful stew that's perfect for a cold day. While it may not be as well-known internationally, it's a dish that offers a true taste of regional German cuisine.

**Where to Savor Hearty Winter Dishes**
For a traditional German soup or stew, visit one of Berlin's cozy restaurants or food stalls at the Christmas markets. At the Alexanderplatz Christmas Market, you'll find vendors serving up steaming bowls of Kartoffelsuppe, often with a variety of toppings to choose from. If you're looking for a sit-down meal, head to a traditional German restaurant like Zur Letzten Instanz, Berlin's oldest restaurant, where you can enjoy a range of hearty winter dishes in a historic setting.

# 4.2 International Holiday Cuisine

Berlin's diverse culinary scene means that you're not limited to traditional German fare during the holiday season. The city is home to a wide array of international restaurants that offer festive dishes from around the world, allowing you to explore global flavors without leaving the city.

### Italian Christmas at Muntagnola

### A Taste of Italy in Berlin
For those craving Italian cuisine during the Christmas season, Muntagnola offers a warm and inviting atmosphere where you can enjoy traditional Italian dishes with a holiday twist. Located in the heart of Berlin, this family-run restaurant specializes in the flavors of Southern Italy, using fresh ingredients to create dishes that are both authentic and delicious.

During the Christmas season, Muntagnola offers a special holiday menu that features classic Italian dishes such as **Tortellini in Brodo** (pasta stuffed with meat or cheese, served in a rich broth), **Porchetta** (roast pork with herbs), and a variety of seafood dishes that are a staple of Italian Christmas Eve dinners. For dessert, indulge in **Panettone** or **Pandoro**, traditional Italian Christmas cakes that are light, airy, and full of flavor.

### Why Muntagnola Stands Out
Muntagnola is not just about the food; it's about the experience. The restaurant's cozy interior, decorated with festive lights and ornaments, creates a perfect setting for a holiday meal. The staff is friendly and knowledgeable, making you feel like part of the family. Whether you're dining with a large group or looking for a

romantic dinner for two, Muntagnola offers an unforgettable Italian Christmas experience in the heart of Berlin.

## French Delicacies at La Bonne Franquette

### An Elegant French Christmas

La Bonne Franquette brings the elegance and sophistication of French cuisine to Berlin, offering a delightful escape into the world of Parisian dining. This charming bistro is known for its traditional French dishes, prepared with a focus on quality ingredients and classic techniques.

During the holiday season, La Bonne Franquette's menu includes festive favorites such as **Foie Gras**, **Coquilles Saint-Jacques** (scallops in a creamy sauce), and **Duck à l'Orange**. For dessert, the restaurant serves **Bûche de Noël**, a traditional French Christmas cake shaped like a yule log, made with rich chocolate sponge and buttercream.

### The Perfect French Dining Experience

Dining at La Bonne Franquette during the Christmas season is a treat for the senses. The restaurant's warm, intimate setting, complete with candlelit tables and tasteful holiday decorations, provides the perfect backdrop for a festive meal. The attentive service and extensive wine list, featuring selections from France's best vineyards, ensure a dining experience that is both refined and memorable.

# Scandinavian Flavors at Munch's Hus

### A Nordic Christmas in Berlin

For a taste of Scandinavia during the holiday season, Munch's Hus offers a menu inspired by the flavors of Norway, Sweden, and Denmark. This restaurant is a favorite among locals and visitors alike, known for its hearty, rustic dishes that showcase the best of Nordic cuisine.

The Christmas menu at Munch's Hus features traditional Scandinavian dishes such as **Gravlax** (cured salmon), **Julebords** (a festive buffet with a variety of cold and warm dishes), and **Ribbe** (roast pork belly with crackling). The restaurant also offers a selection of Nordic desserts, including **Risalamande** (a Danish rice pudding with almonds) and **Lussekatter** (Swedish saffron buns).

### Why Munch's Hus Is a Must-Visit

Munch's Hus is more than just a restaurant; it's a celebration of Nordic culture. The cozy, wood-paneled interior, complete with traditional Scandinavian decorations, creates a warm and inviting atmosphere that's perfect for a holiday meal. The friendly staff, dressed in traditional Nordic attire, add to the authenticity of the experience, making Munch's Hus a must-visit destination for anyone looking to explore Scandinavian Christmas traditions in Berlin.

# 4.3 Best Cafés and Restaurants for a Cozy Christmas Meal

Berlin is home to a wide range of cafés and restaurants that offer the perfect setting for a cozy Christmas meal. Whether you're looking for a quiet place to enjoy a cup of coffee and a slice of cake, or a fine dining experience to celebrate the holidays, the city has something to suit every taste.

### Café Einstein Stammhaus

### A Berlin Institution
Café Einstein Stammhaus is one of Berlin's most iconic cafés, known for its elegant Viennese-style interiors and a menu that offers a mix of German and Austrian classics. Located in a beautiful old villa in the Tiergarten district, this café has been a favorite among locals and tourists alike for decades.

During the Christmas season, Café Einstein Stammhaus is beautifully decorated with festive lights and ornaments, creating a warm and inviting atmosphere. The menu includes a variety of seasonal specialties, such as **Apfelstrudel** (apple strudel), **Sachertorte** (a rich chocolate cake), and a selection of holiday cookies. Pair these treats with a cup of their famous coffee, and you have the perfect recipe for a cozy afternoon.

### Why Café Einstein Stammhaus Is Special
What sets Café Einstein Stammhaus apart is its

combination of historical charm and modern comfort. The café's grand interiors, complete with high ceilings, chandeliers, and wood-paneled walls, transport you back to a bygone era, while the friendly service and high-quality offerings ensure a contemporary dining experience. It's the perfect place to relax and enjoy a leisurely meal or a quick coffee break during your holiday explorations in Berlin.

**Restaurant Tim Raue**

### Fine Dining at Its Best

For those looking to celebrate Christmas with a fine dining experience, Restaurant Tim Raue offers an unparalleled culinary journey. Run by renowned chef Tim Raue, this Michelin-starred restaurant is known for its innovative fusion of Asian and European flavors, creating dishes that are both bold and sophisticated.

The holiday menu at Restaurant Tim Raue features a selection of exquisite dishes that showcase the chef's creativity and attention to detail. From **Peking Duck** with German influences to **Japanese-inspired sashimi**, each dish is a work of art, both in presentation and taste. The restaurant's extensive wine list, curated by sommelier André Macionga, ensures the perfect pairing for every course.

### An Unforgettable Dining Experience

Dining at Restaurant Tim Raue is an experience that goes beyond the food. The restaurant's sleek, modern interiors, combined with impeccable service, create an atmosphere of luxury and refinement. Whether you're celebrating a special occasion or simply want to treat yourself to an unforgettable meal, Restaurant Tim Raue is the place to be.

## Rutz Wine Bar

### A Wine Lover's Paradise
Rutz Wine Bar is a must-visit destination for wine enthusiasts, offering an impressive selection of wines from around the world, paired with a menu of creative and seasonal dishes. Located in the Mitte district, this wine bar is known for its relaxed yet sophisticated atmosphere, making it a perfect spot for a cozy Christmas meal.

The menu at Rutz Wine Bar changes regularly to reflect the best seasonal ingredients, with a focus on modern European cuisine. During the Christmas season, you can expect dishes like **Venison with Cranberries**, **Truffled Potato Soup**, and **Chestnut Risotto**, all designed to complement the extensive wine list. The knowledgeable staff are always on hand to recommend the perfect wine pairing for your meal, ensuring a dining experience that is both enjoyable and educational.

### Why Rutz Wine Bar Is a Must-Visit
Rutz Wine Bar's combination of excellent food, an outstanding wine selection, and a cozy, welcoming atmosphere make it a top choice for a Christmas meal in

Berlin. Whether you're a seasoned wine connoisseur or simply looking to enjoy a festive dinner with friends or family, Rutz Wine Bar offers an experience that is both relaxed and refined.

# Chapter 5: Shopping in Berlin: From Luxury to Local Crafts

Berlin is a city that offers a unique shopping experience, blending the best of luxury, avant-garde design, and traditional craftsmanship. During the Christmas season, the city transforms into a shopper's paradise, with its streets, malls, and markets brimming with festive cheer. Whether you're looking to indulge in high-end shopping, discover one-of-a-kind artisan goods, or simply soak in the holiday atmosphere, Berlin has something for everyone. In this chapter, we'll explore the top shopping destinations, highlight the best Christmas boutiques and artisan markets, and provide useful tips for tax-free shopping and gift wrapping.

## 5.1 Top Shopping Destinations

Berlin's shopping landscape is as diverse as the city itself. From iconic department stores and concept malls to high-end shopping boulevards, the city offers a range of options to suit every style and budget.

### KaDeWe: Berlin's Iconic Department Store

### The Ultimate Shopping Experience

Kaufhaus des Westens, better known as KaDeWe, is not just a department store—it's an institution. Located on Tauentzienstraße, near the bustling Kurfürstendamm, KaDeWe has been a symbol of luxury and elegance in

Berlin since its opening in 1907. It's the largest department store in continental Europe, boasting over 60,000 square meters of retail space spread across eight floors.

During the Christmas season, KaDeWe is transformed into a winter wonderland, with lavish decorations, festive displays, and an array of seasonal merchandise. The ground floor is dedicated to luxury fashion and accessories, featuring brands like Chanel, Dior, and Louis Vuitton. As you move up the floors, you'll find everything from home decor and beauty products to gourmet food and wine.

**A Gourmet Heaven**
One of the highlights of KaDeWe is its legendary sixth-floor food hall, known as the "Feinschmeckeretage." Here, you can indulge in an array of gourmet delights, from fresh seafood and fine cheeses to exquisite pastries and chocolates. During the holiday season, the food hall offers a special selection of Christmas treats, including handcrafted marzipan, stollen, and specialty wines. It's the perfect place to pick up festive gifts or to simply treat yourself to something delicious.

**Why KaDeWe Is a Must-Visit**
A visit to KaDeWe is more than just a shopping trip—it's an experience. The store's opulent interiors, combined with its wide selection of luxury goods, make it a must-visit destination for anyone in Berlin. Whether

you're looking to splurge on a designer handbag, pick up gourmet delicacies, or simply marvel at the festive decorations, KaDeWe offers something for everyone.

## Bikini Berlin: A Concept Mall Experience

### Innovative Shopping in the Heart of Berlin

Bikini Berlin is not your typical shopping mall. Located in the City West district, near the Berlin Zoo, this concept mall offers a unique blend of retail, dining, and entertainment, all within a striking architectural setting. The building itself is a mid-century modern gem, with large windows that offer stunning views of the zoo's monkey enclosure—hence the name "Bikini."

What sets Bikini Berlin apart is its focus on creativity and innovation. The mall is home to a curated selection of boutique stores, pop-up shops, and concept spaces, many of which feature local and emerging designers. This makes it the perfect place to discover unique, one-of-a-kind items that you won't find anywhere else.

### A Creative Hub

Bikini Berlin is more than just a shopping destination—it's a cultural hub. The mall hosts regular art exhibitions, fashion shows, and events that draw in a creative crowd. During the Christmas season, Bikini Berlin comes alive with festive activities, including live music, art installations, and special holiday pop-ups.

### Why Bikini Berlin Is Worth a Visit

If you're looking for a shopping experience that's a little

out of the ordinary, Bikini Berlin is the place to be. The mall's mix of fashion, art, and design makes it a must-visit for anyone interested in Berlin's creative scene. Plus, its location near the Berlin Zoo and Tiergarten makes it an ideal stop during a day of sightseeing.

## Friedrichstraße: High-End Shopping Boulevard

### A Stroll Down Berlin's Luxury Avenue
Friedrichstraße is one of Berlin's most famous shopping streets, known for its high-end boutiques, luxury brands, and elegant department stores. Stretching from Checkpoint Charlie to Friedrichstadt-Palast, this boulevard is a haven for fashionistas and luxury shoppers.

During the Christmas season, Friedrichstraße is beautifully decorated with festive lights and window displays, creating a magical atmosphere that's perfect for holiday shopping. The street is home to a variety of designer boutiques, including names like Gucci, Prada, and Hugo Boss, as well as upscale department stores like Galeries Lafayette.

### The French Touch
Galeries Lafayette, located on Friedrichstraße, brings a touch of Parisian chic to Berlin. This upscale department store offers a carefully curated selection of fashion, beauty, and gourmet products, with a focus on French brands. The store's food hall, located in the basement, is

a must-visit for anyone looking to indulge in fine wines, cheeses, and pastries. During the holiday season, Galeries Lafayette offers a range of exclusive Christmas products, making it a great place to pick up gifts for loved ones.

**Why Friedrichstraße Is a Shopping Hotspot**
Friedrichstraße offers the quintessential luxury shopping experience in Berlin. Its mix of designer boutiques, department stores, and gourmet shops makes it a top destination for those looking to indulge in some high-end retail therapy. Whether you're shopping for the perfect Christmas outfit or searching for luxury gifts, Friedrichstraße has something to offer.

# 5.2 Christmas Boutiques and Artisan Markets

Berlin's Christmas markets are famous for their festive atmosphere, but they're also a great place to find unique, handcrafted gifts. In addition to the traditional markets, Berlin is home to a variety of Christmas boutiques and artisan markets that offer a more curated shopping experience.

**Christmas at the Hackescher Markt**

**A Festive Market with a Bohemian Flair**
Located in the trendy Mitte district, the Hackescher Markt Christmas market is a favorite among locals and tourists alike. This small but charming market offers a

unique blend of traditional holiday cheer and modern, bohemian vibes, making it a must-visit for anyone looking to experience Berlin's creative side.

The market's stalls are filled with handmade crafts, artisanal foods, and unique gifts, many of which are created by local artists and designers. From hand-knitted scarves and hats to beautifully crafted jewelry and home decor, the Hackescher Markt Christmas market is the perfect place to find one-of-a-kind gifts for friends and family.

**Live Music and Entertainment**
In addition to its shopping offerings, the Hackescher Markt Christmas market also features live music and entertainment, adding to the festive atmosphere. Whether you're sipping on a cup of hot mulled wine or browsing the stalls, the market's lively ambiance is sure to put you in the holiday spirit.

**Why Hackescher Markt Stands Out**
The Hackescher Markt Christmas market is not just about shopping—it's about the experience. Its unique blend of traditional and modern elements, combined with its vibrant atmosphere, makes it a must-visit for anyone looking to experience a different side of Berlin's Christmas markets.

**Designer Boutiques in Mitte**
**A Hub for Berlin's Fashion Scene**
Mitte is the heart of Berlin's fashion scene, home to a wide range of designer boutiques that offer everything

from cutting-edge fashion to timeless classics. During the Christmas season, these boutiques are filled with festive collections, making them the perfect place to shop for stylish holiday outfits or luxury gifts.

One of the highlights of shopping in Mitte is the variety of independent boutiques that showcase the work of local and emerging designers. Stores like The Corner Berlin and Andreas Murkudis offer a curated selection of high-end fashion, accessories, and home decor, with a focus on quality and craftsmanship.

### Why Mitte Is a Fashion Lover's Paradise

Mitte's designer boutiques offer a shopping experience that's both exclusive and inspiring. Whether you're looking to discover the latest trends or invest in a timeless piece, the district's boutiques offer something for every fashion lover. Plus, the area's stylish cafes and restaurants provide the perfect setting for a post-shopping break.

### Vintage Shopping in Kreuzberg

### A Treasure Trove of Retro Finds

For those who love the thrill of the hunt, Kreuzberg is the place to be. This vibrant neighborhood is known for its eclectic mix of vintage shops and flea markets, where you can find everything from retro fashion to antique furniture. Whether you're looking for a unique piece of clothing or a quirky gift, Kreuzberg's vintage scene offers a shopping experience like no other.

One of the best places to start your vintage shopping adventure is at the Nowkoelln Flowmarkt, a popular flea market that takes place along the banks of the Landwehr Canal. Here, you'll find a wide range of second-hand goods, including vintage clothing, vinyl records, and handmade crafts. The market's laid-back atmosphere and scenic location make it a great place to spend a Sunday afternoon.

### Why Vintage Shopping in Kreuzberg Is a Must-Do

Kreuzberg's vintage shops and flea markets offer a shopping experience that's both fun and rewarding. The neighborhood's bohemian vibe, combined with its wide range of retro finds, makes it a top destination for anyone looking to add a unique touch to their holiday shopping.

## 5.3 Tips for Tax-Free Shopping and Gift Wrapping

Shopping in Berlin during the holiday season is a delight, and with a few tips, you can make the most of your experience. From understanding VAT refunds to finding the best places to get your gifts wrapped, this section will help you navigate the ins and outs of shopping in Berlin.

### Understanding VAT Refunds

### How to Shop Tax-Free

As a non-EU resident, you're eligible for a VAT refund on

many of your purchases in Berlin. VAT (Value Added Tax) is typically included in the price of goods, and the refund process allows you to reclaim a portion of that tax, making your shopping even more affordable.

To take advantage of the VAT refund, you'll need to make sure that the store you're shopping at participates in the refund scheme. Most major department stores and boutiques offer this service, and you'll need to spend a minimum amount (usually around €25) in a single store to qualify.

**The Refund Process**
When making a purchase, ask the retailer for a VAT refund form. You'll need to fill out this form and keep your receipt. When you leave the EU, you'll need to present the form, receipt, and purchased goods to customs at the airport or border, where they will stamp your form. After that, you can claim your refund at a designated refund counter or by mailing the stamped form back to the retailer or refund agency.

**Why VAT Refunds Are Worth the Effort**
While the VAT refund process can seem a bit cumbersome, it's worth the effort, especially if you're making large purchases. The refund can be anywhere from 7% to 19% of your purchase price, depending on the item, which can add up to significant savings.

## Where to Get Gifts Wrapped

### Adding a Personal Touch
Once you've found the perfect gifts, the next step is to get them beautifully wrapped. Many stores in Berlin offer gift-wrapping services, especially during the holiday season. Department stores like KaDeWe and Galeries Lafayette provide complimentary wrapping for your purchases, with a variety of festive papers and ribbons to choose from.

If you prefer a more personalized touch, there are also several specialty shops in Berlin that offer custom gift-wrapping services. These shops often use high-quality papers and unique embellishments, ensuring that your gifts look as special as the contents inside.

### DIY Gift Wrapping
For those who enjoy getting creative, there are plenty of stores in Berlin that sell beautiful wrapping papers, ribbons, and gift tags. Stores like Paper & Tea in Mitte and Modulor in Kreuzberg offer a wide range of stylish and unique wrapping supplies. You can also find eco-friendly options, such as recycled paper and reusable fabric wraps, which are both stylish and sustainable.

### Why Gift Wrapping Matters
Beautifully wrapped gifts add an extra layer of thoughtfulness to your presents, making them even

more special for the recipient. Whether you choose to have your gifts professionally wrapped or do it yourself, taking the time to wrap your gifts nicely is a small gesture that goes a long way.

## Shipping Gifts Home

### Hassle-Free Shipping

If you're worried about fitting all your holiday purchases into your luggage, shipping gifts home is a convenient option. Many stores in Berlin offer shipping services, allowing you to send your gifts directly to your loved ones or to your home. This is especially useful for larger or more fragile items, such as glass ornaments or bulky clothing.

When shipping gifts, make sure to ask the retailer about insurance options to protect your items in transit. It's also a good idea to check the shipping times and costs, especially if you're sending gifts internationally. During the busy holiday season, shipping times can be longer than usual, so plan ahead to ensure your gifts arrive on time.

### Why Shipping Can Be a Lifesaver

Shipping your gifts home can save you the hassle of carrying extra luggage, and it also ensures that your purchases are safely delivered to your destination. Whether you're sending gifts to friends and family or simply lightening your load for the trip home, shipping is a convenient and stress-free option.

Shopping in Berlin during the Christmas season is a magical experience, offering a blend of luxury, creativity, and tradition. From the opulence of KaDeWe to the bohemian charm of Hackescher Markt, the city's shopping destinations cater to every taste and budget. With the added benefits of tax-free shopping, professional gift-wrapping services, and convenient shipping options, your holiday shopping in Berlin is sure to be both enjoyable and rewarding. Whether you're treating yourself or searching for the perfect gifts for your loved ones, Berlin's vibrant shopping scene has everything you need to make this Christmas truly special.

# Chapter 6: Experiencing Berlin's Winter Wonderland Outdoors

Winter in Berlin offers a unique charm, transforming the city into a picturesque landscape of snow-covered parks, twinkling Christmas lights, and serene, frozen waterfalls. The colder months provide a different perspective on Berlin's outdoor spaces, showcasing their beauty and tranquility. Whether you're looking to take a leisurely stroll through snow-dusted gardens or marvel at festive light displays, Berlin's winter wonderland has something for everyone. In this chapter, we'll explore the city's parks and gardens in their winter splendor, including Tiergarten, the Botanical Garden, and Viktoriapark, highlighting the best ways to experience their seasonal magic.

## 6.1 Parks and Gardens in Winter

Berlin's parks and gardens offer an enchanting escape from the hustle and bustle of the city, particularly during the winter months. The crisp, cold air and serene landscapes create a tranquil setting for outdoor activities and leisurely explorations. Here are three must-visit spots to experience Berlin's winter wonderland:

### Tiergarten's Snow-Covered Beauty

### A Classic Winter Stroll
Tiergarten is Berlin's largest and most famous park,

offering a vast expanse of greenery in the heart of the city. During winter, the park transforms into a snowy landscape, with its winding paths and open spaces blanketed in a soft layer of white. This vast urban oasis is perfect for a winter stroll, allowing you to enjoy the beauty of nature while being surrounded by the city's historic landmarks.

One of the highlights of Tiergarten in winter is the opportunity to witness the park's classic features under a fresh layer of snow. The park's many ponds and lakes, such as the Neuer See, take on a serene, almost magical quality as they freeze over, providing a stunning contrast to the white snow. The park's statues and monuments, including the iconic Victory Column, become striking focal points against the snowy backdrop, offering fantastic photo opportunities.

**Winter Activities**
While Tiergarten is ideal for peaceful walks, it also offers a range of winter activities. The park's wide paths are perfect for cross-country skiing or snowshoeing, should the conditions be right. If you're visiting with children, the park's open spaces are great for building snowmen or having snowball fights. Additionally, the park's many cafés and kiosks, such as the Café am Neuen See, provide a warm refuge where you can enjoy a hot drink and a snack while taking in the winter scenery.

**Why Tiergarten is a Winter Must-Visit**
Tiergarten's expansive grounds and central location

make it a perfect spot to experience Berlin's winter beauty. Its combination of historic landmarks, picturesque landscapes, and outdoor activities ensure that there's something for everyone, whether you're looking for a quiet retreat or an active winter adventure.

**Botanical Garden's Christmas Lights**

**A Festive Wonderland**

The Berlin Botanical Garden, located in the southwestern part of the city, is renowned for its diverse plant collections and beautifully designed landscapes. During the winter months, the garden becomes a festive wonderland, thanks to its enchanting Christmas lights display. The annual "Christmas Garden" event transforms the garden into a magical spectacle of lights, with intricate illuminations that highlight the park's natural beauty.

The Christmas Garden features a winding light trail that guides visitors through the park's various sections, including the historic greenhouse complex and the garden's expansive grounds. The light displays include sparkling trees, glowing arches, and shimmering ponds, creating a fairy-tale atmosphere that's perfect for a winter evening stroll. The event typically runs from late November through early January, offering plenty of time to enjoy the holiday magic.

**Additional Attractions**

In addition to the Christmas lights, the Botanical Garden

offers a range of winter activities and attractions. The garden's tropical greenhouse, which houses exotic plants from around the world, provides a warm and inviting escape from the cold. The café on-site offers a selection of seasonal treats and hot beverages, allowing you to relax and warm up after exploring the light displays.

### Why the Botanical Garden is Worth a Visit
The Berlin Botanical Garden's Christmas Garden event is a must-see for anyone visiting Berlin during the winter season. The combination of stunning light displays, unique plant collections, and festive atmosphere makes it a memorable experience for visitors of all ages.

### Viktoriapark and its Frozen Waterfalls

### A Hidden Gem in Winter
Viktoriapark, located in the Kreuzberg district, is one of Berlin's lesser-known parks, but it offers a unique and picturesque winter experience. The park is renowned for its artificial waterfall, which becomes a breathtaking frozen feature during the colder months. The combination of the cascading ice and the surrounding snowy landscape creates a striking contrast, making it a hidden gem in Berlin's winter scenery.

### Exploring the Frozen Waterfall
The park's waterfall is the focal point of the winter landscape, with its icy flow creating a stunning natural sculpture. The surrounding park area, with its gently

rolling hills and scenic viewpoints, provides ample opportunities for winter walks and photo sessions. The park's elevated position also offers panoramic views of the city, adding to the park's allure.

**Winter Activities**
Viktoriapark's snow-covered slopes are perfect for sledding or tobogganing, providing fun for families and children. The park's peaceful atmosphere makes it an ideal spot for a winter picnic or simply enjoying the serene beauty of the frozen waterfall. The nearby café, situated at the park's entrance, offers a cozy place to warm up with a hot drink and a bite to eat.

**Why Viktoriapark is a Winter Favorite**
Viktoriapark's combination of a frozen waterfall, panoramic views, and tranquil setting makes it a standout destination for experiencing Berlin's winter charm. Its less crowded nature compared to other parks allows for a more relaxed and intimate winter experience.

# 6.2 Outdoor Winter Sports and Activities

Winter in Berlin reveals a different side of the city, transforming it into a playground of snow-dusted parks, festive events, and a variety of outdoor activities. Embracing the cold and immersing yourself in Berlin's winter magic offers a unique experience, from skating on frozen rinks to exploring historical sites under a blanket of snow. This chapter delves into Berlin's outdoor winter sports and activities, including ice skating, tobogganing, and cross-country skiing, as well as guided winter walks and tours that showcase the city's charm and history during the colder months.

Berlin offers a range of outdoor activities that take advantage of its winter weather, whether you're looking for a thrilling adventure or a relaxing way to enjoy the season. Here's a guide to some of the best winter sports and activities in the city:

## Ice Skating Rinks Across the City

### Classic Ice Skating Venues

Ice skating is a quintessential winter activity, and Berlin has several picturesque rinks where you can glide across the ice amidst festive surroundings. Each rink offers a unique atmosphere, ranging from traditional settings to modern designs.

1. **Berliner Weihnachtszeit at Alexanderplatz**
   The ice rink at Alexanderplatz, set against the backdrop of the iconic TV Tower, is one of Berlin's most popular winter attractions. This rink is part of the Berliner Weihnachtszeit Christmas market, which transforms the square into a festive wonderland. The rink's central location makes it easily accessible and perfect for a day of skating followed by exploring the market's stalls and enjoying seasonal treats.

2. **Ice World at Potsdamer Platz**

   Potsdamer Platz, a major entertainment and shopping district, hosts the Ice World, a sprawling ice rink that extends over 3,000 square meters. The rink is beautifully illuminated and surrounded by festive decorations, creating a magical winter atmosphere. The Ice World also features an ice slide for added fun, making it a great spot for families and friends to enjoy.

3. **Zukunft am Gleisdreieck**

   For a more contemporary skating experience, the Zukunft rink at Gleisdreieck Park offers a modern, urban setting. This rink is known for its sleek design and lively atmosphere, often featuring DJs and live music events. It's a fantastic option if you're looking for a vibrant, social skating experience.

### Ice Skating Tips

When visiting Berlin's ice rinks, consider renting skates on-site if you don't have your own. Many rinks offer rental services, and it's a good idea to wear warm clothing and gloves to stay comfortable. If you're new to ice skating, taking a few lessons or practicing on less crowded days can help you gain confidence.

### Tobogganing at Teufelsberg

### A Thrilling Winter Adventure

Teufelsberg, an artificial hill made from rubble and debris from World War II, is one of Berlin's best spots for tobogganing. Located in the Grunewald forest, this former listening station provides a steep slope perfect for sledding and tobogganing. The hill's height and the surrounding forest create an exhilarating winter experience, with panoramic views of the city offering a stunning backdrop.

## What to Bring
If you're planning to go tobogganing at Teufelsberg, bring your own sled or toboggan, as rentals are not typically available on-site. Warm, waterproof clothing is essential, as well as sturdy footwear to navigate the snowy terrain. For safety, always be mindful of other sledders and follow any posted guidelines.

## Why Teufelsberg is Special
Teufelsberg's combination of thrilling slopes and scenic views makes it a unique winter destination. The hill's history and location in the forest add to its charm, offering a blend of outdoor adventure and natural beauty.

## Cross-Country Skiing in Grunewald Forest

## Exploring Berlin's Largest Forest
Grunewald Forest, located in the southwestern part of Berlin, is an expansive area that offers excellent opportunities for cross-country skiing. The forest's network of trails winds through scenic woodlands and along frozen lakes, providing a serene setting for skiing.

### Popular Trails and Routes

Several trails in Grunewald are well-suited for cross-country skiing, including routes around the Schlachtensee and the Wannsee. These trails offer varying levels of difficulty, catering to both beginners and experienced skiers. The forest's tranquil atmosphere and scenic views make it an ideal location for a winter sports adventure.

### What to Know Before You Go

If you're new to cross-country skiing, consider renting equipment and taking a lesson to familiarize yourself with the technique. Grunewald's trails are generally well-maintained, but checking current conditions before heading out is a good idea. Ensure you dress in layers and wear appropriate ski gear to stay warm and comfortable.

## 6.3 Guided Winter Walks and Tours

Guided winter walks and tours offer a fantastic way to explore Berlin's history, culture, and hidden gems during the colder months. From historical tours with a festive twist to ghost walks and bicycle tours, these experiences provide a unique perspective on the city's winter charm.

### Historical Walking Tours with a Holiday Twist

### Exploring Berlin's Past During the Festive Season

Berlin's history is rich and multifaceted, and exploring it

during the winter months adds an extra layer of charm. Many tour operators offer historical walking tours that focus on different aspects of Berlin's past while incorporating seasonal elements.

1. **Old Berlin Walking Tour**
   This tour takes you through Berlin's historic center, highlighting key landmarks and neighborhoods from the city's past. During the holiday season, the tour often includes stops at festive markets and historic buildings decorated for Christmas, providing a blend of history and holiday cheer.
2. **Christmas in Berlin Tour**
   Focusing specifically on the city's Christmas traditions, this tour explores the origins of Berlin's holiday customs and their evolution over the years. Participants visit historical sites associated with Berlin's Christmas history, including traditional markets and famous Christmas landmarks.

**Why Historical Tours Are a Great Option**

Historical walking tours offer a deep dive into Berlin's past while allowing you to experience the city's festive atmosphere. They provide context for the city's landmarks and traditions, making them a valuable addition to your winter itinerary.

# Ghost Walks in Berlin's Dark History

## A Spooky Winter Adventure

Berlin's history is filled with dark and mysterious tales, and ghost walks offer a spine-tingling way to explore the city's haunted past. These tours guide you through eerie locations and share stories of ghosts and legends that have become part of Berlin's folklore.

1. **Berlin Ghost Tour**
   This popular tour takes you through some of Berlin's most haunted locations, including historic buildings and shadowy alleyways. The guides share chilling tales of ghostly encounters and supernatural events, adding a thrilling dimension to your winter exploration.

2. **Dark History Walking Tour**
   Focusing on Berlin's darker historical moments, this tour explores the city's more somber past, including tales of war and espionage. The winter setting adds an atmospheric touch, making it a compelling option for those interested in the city's historical mysteries.

## Why Ghost Walks Are Unique

Ghost walks provide a different perspective on Berlin's history, combining historical facts with local legends. They offer a unique and engaging way to explore the city's past, making them a memorable addition to your winter visit.

**Bicycle Tours of Winter Berlin**
**Exploring Berlin on Two Wheels**
While winter in Berlin may be cold, it's also a great time to explore the city by bicycle. Several tour operators offer winter bicycle tours that take you through Berlin's neighborhoods and landmarks, providing a unique and active way to see the city.

1. **Berlin Highlights Bicycle Tour**
   This tour covers key landmarks and neighborhoods, offering a comprehensive overview of Berlin's attractions. During the winter months, the tour often includes stops at festive markets and seasonal events, allowing you to experience the city's winter charm while staying active.

2. **Winter Wonderland Bicycle Tour**
   Focusing specifically on Berlin's winter scenery, this tour takes you through parks, gardens, and snowy streets, showcasing the city's seasonal beauty. The tour is designed to be comfortable and enjoyable despite the cold, with frequent stops to warm up and take in the sights.

**Why Bicycle Tours Are Enjoyable in Winter**
Bicycle tours provide a dynamic way to explore Berlin, allowing you to cover more ground and see the city from a different perspective. With the right gear and clothing, cycling in winter can be a pleasant and invigorating experience, offering a unique way to enjoy Berlin's winter landscape.

# Chapter 7: Staying Stress-Free During the Holidays in Berlin

Visiting Berlin during the Christmas season is a magical experience, but it can also come with its share of challenges. From navigating the bustling holiday crowds to staying warm and healthy, proper planning can help ensure that your trip is as enjoyable and stress-free as possible. In this chapter, we'll cover essential tips for planning your trip, avoiding crowds, and staying safe and comfortable during Berlin's winter months.

## 7.1 Planning Your Trip: Essential Tips

### Booking Flights and Accommodations Early

#### Why Early Booking is Crucial
Booking your flights and accommodations well in advance is one of the most effective ways to ensure a smooth and stress-free trip. The Christmas season is a peak travel period, and Berlin is a popular destination due to its festive markets, holiday lights, and seasonal events. Early booking helps secure better rates and availability, avoiding the last-minute rush and potential disappointments.

#### Flights
When booking flights to Berlin, consider flying into Berlin Brandenburg Airport (BER), the city's main international airport. To get the best deals, book your tickets at least

three to four months before your planned departure. Use flight comparison websites to find the most competitive prices and flexible dates. Additionally, booking mid-week flights can sometimes offer better rates than weekend departures.

## Accommodations

Berlin offers a wide range of accommodation options, from luxury hotels to budget-friendly hostels and vacation rentals. Popular areas to stay during the Christmas season include Mitte, which is central and close to many attractions, and Charlottenburg, known for its elegant charm and proximity to the Christmas markets at Charlottenburg Palace. For a more local experience, consider neighborhoods like Prenzlauer Berg or Kreuzberg.

## Best Time to Book

Ideally, book your accommodations as soon as you have your travel dates confirmed. Christmas and New Year's are busy times, and hotels and rentals can fill up quickly. Early booking ensures you have a wider selection of options and better rates. Additionally, many hotels offer early-bird discounts or special holiday packages that can enhance your stay.

## Best Time to Visit Berlin During Christmas

## When to Go for the Best Experience

Berlin is known for its festive atmosphere during the Christmas season, which generally runs from late

November to early January. The best time to visit depends on your preferences for weather, crowds, and events.

### Early December

Visiting Berlin in early December allows you to enjoy the city's Christmas markets and decorations before the peak holiday rush. The crowds are typically smaller, and you can explore the markets and attractions more leisurely. This is also a good time for enjoying pre-Christmas events and shopping without the stress of last-minute holiday shoppers.

### Mid to Late December

The holiday season reaches its peak from mid-December to Christmas Eve, with bustling markets, crowded attractions, and a vibrant atmosphere. If you enjoy a festive, bustling environment, this is the time to experience the full range of Christmas festivities. However, be prepared for larger crowds and higher prices.

### After Christmas

Visiting Berlin after Christmas and before New Year's Eve offers a quieter experience. Many of the Christmas markets remain open until early January, and you can still enjoy the holiday lights and seasonal activities. This period is ideal for those who prefer a more relaxed experience and want to avoid the busiest times.

## Navigating Berlin's Public Transport System

### Understanding Berlin's Transport Network
Berlin's public transport system is efficient and easy to navigate, making it simple to get around the city during your visit. The system includes buses, trams, trains (S-Bahn and U-Bahn), and ferries, all integrated into one cohesive network.

### Buying Tickets
Tickets for public transport can be purchased at kiosks, ticket machines, or via mobile apps. Single-journey tickets, day passes, and multi-day passes are available, with prices varying depending on the number of zones you plan to travel through. For tourists, a Berlin WelcomeCard offers unlimited travel on public transport and discounts at various attractions.

### Using Public Transport
To use the public transport system, simply validate your ticket at the start of your journey by stamping it at the designated machines. Be sure to check the schedule and routes in advance, especially during the holiday season when services might be affected by increased passenger volumes and holiday schedules.

### Transport Tips

- **Plan Ahead**: Use apps like BVG or Google Maps to plan your routes and check real-time schedules.

- **Travel Off-Peak**: If possible, avoid peak travel times (typically early mornings and late afternoons) to avoid crowded trains and buses.
- **Keep Essentials Handy**: Carry your ticket, a map of the transport network, and any necessary contact information for easy access.

# 7.2 Avoiding Crowds and Long Lines

### Early Morning vs. Late Night Visits

### Best Times to Explore
Visiting popular attractions and Christmas markets early in the morning or late at night can help you avoid the busiest times. The early hours typically offer a quieter experience, with fewer crowds and shorter lines. Similarly, many attractions are less crowded in the evening, and the holiday lights create a beautiful atmosphere after dark.

### Christmas Markets
Arriving at Christmas markets right when they open can help you enjoy the stalls and food without the long lines that build up later in the day. Additionally, many markets are open until late in the evening, providing an alternative time to visit if you prefer a more relaxed atmosphere.

### Attractions
For popular attractions like the Berlin Cathedral, the Reichstag, or museums, consider visiting early in the

day or late in the afternoon. Weekdays are generally less crowded than weekends, and booking tickets in advance can also help you avoid long lines.

## Skip-the-Line Tickets for Attractions

### Advantages of Skip-the-Line Options
Many of Berlin's popular attractions offer skip-the-line tickets, which allow you to bypass the long queues and enter the site at a designated time. These tickets can be a valuable investment, especially during the busy holiday season.

### Where to Buy
Skip-the-line tickets can often be purchased online through the attraction's official website or through third-party booking platforms. Booking in advance ensures you secure your entry time and avoid the frustration of waiting in long lines.

### How to Use
When you arrive at the attraction, proceed to the designated entrance for skip-the-line tickets. Make sure to bring a copy of your booking confirmation, either printed or on your mobile device, to present at the entrance.

## Off-the-Beaten-Path Experiences

### Exploring Lesser-Known Attractions
In addition to the major attractions and Christmas markets, Berlin offers a wealth of off-the-beaten-path

experiences that can provide a more relaxed and unique perspective on the city. Exploring lesser-known sites can also help you avoid the crowds.

## Hidden Gems

1. **Museum of Photography**: Located in the Kulturforum, this museum showcases the works of famous photographers and offers a more intimate museum experience.
2. **Prenzlauer Berg**: This neighborhood features charming streets, independent shops, and cozy cafés, providing a more laid-back atmosphere compared to the tourist-heavy areas.
3. **Kreuzberg's Street Art**: Take a self-guided tour of the street art and murals in Kreuzberg, where you can discover Berlin's vibrant artistic scene away from the main tourist spots.

## Seasonal Activities

- **Winter Walks**: Explore Berlin's lesser-known parks and green spaces, such as the Botanical Garden or the Tiergarten's quieter corners, for a peaceful winter stroll.
- **Local Markets**: Visit smaller, local markets in neighborhoods like Neukölln or Schöneberg for a more authentic shopping experience.

# 7.3 Staying Safe and Warm in Winter

### Dressing for Berlin's Winter Weather

### Understanding the Climate
Berlin's winter weather can be cold and unpredictable, with temperatures ranging from just above freezing to below zero. Snow and rain are common, so it's important to dress appropriately to stay warm and comfortable.

### Layering
Wear multiple layers to stay warm and allow for flexibility in adjusting to changing temperatures. Start with a moisture-wicking base layer to keep sweat away from your skin, followed by an insulating layer like a fleece or sweater, and finish with a waterproof and windproof outer layer.

### Accessories

- **Warm Hat**: A hat helps retain body heat and protect your ears from the cold.
- **Gloves**: Insulated and waterproof gloves are essential for keeping your hands warm and dry.
- **Scarf**: A scarf can protect your neck and face from the cold wind.
- **Warm Footwear**: Insulated and waterproof boots are crucial for walking in snow and slush.

## Tips for Staying Healthy During Your Trip

### Maintaining Health and Well-being

Winter travel can sometimes lead to colds and other illnesses due to the cold weather and exposure to large crowds. Taking a few precautions can help you stay healthy and enjoy your trip to the fullest.

### Hydration and Nutrition

- **Stay Hydrated**: Drink plenty of water to stay hydrated, especially if you're spending a lot of time outdoors.
- **Eat Nutritious Meals**: Enjoy a balanced diet with plenty of fruits and vegetables to keep your immune system strong.

### Health Precautions

- **Wash Your Hands**: Regular handwashing can help prevent the spread of germs and reduce your risk of getting sick.
- **Rest and Relax**: Ensure you get enough rest and avoid overexerting yourself to keep your energy levels up and reduce stress.

### Emergency Contacts and Services

### Important Contacts

Knowing where to turn in case of an emergency can provide peace of mind during your trip. Here are some essential contacts and services:

### Emergency Services

- **Emergency Number**: The emergency number for police, fire, and ambulance services in Germany is 112.
- **Medical Assistance**: For non-emergency medical issues, you can visit a local pharmacy or doctor. Many pharmacies offer basic medical advice and over-the-counter medications.

### Local Contacts

- **Tourist Information Centers**: Berlin has several tourist information centers where you can get assistance, maps, and advice. Locations include the main station (Hauptbahnhof) and Alexanderplatz.
- **Embassies and Consulates**: If you need assistance with passport issues or other consular services, locate your country's embassy or consulate in Berlin.

### Final Tips

- **Emergency Numbers**: Carry a list of emergency contacts, including local emergency services and your accommodation's contact information.
- **Travel Insurance**: Consider purchasing travel insurance that covers health, theft, and trip cancellations for added protection and peace of mind.

Staying stress-free during the holidays in Berlin involves thoughtful planning, understanding the best times to visit, and being prepared for winter weather. By booking your flights and accommodations early, avoiding crowds with smart timing and skip-the-line options, and dressing appropriately for the weather, you can ensure a smooth and enjoyable experience. Navigating Berlin's public transport system efficiently and taking advantage of off-the-beaten-path experiences further enhances your visit. With these tips, you can fully embrace Berlin's winter wonderland and create lasting memories of your holiday trip.

# Chapter 8: Family Fun: Kid-Friendly Activities in Berlin

Berlin is a fantastic destination for families, offering a plethora of activities and attractions that cater to children of all ages. Whether your family enjoys interactive museums, festive events, or indoor adventures, Berlin has something to make your holiday visit both enjoyable and memorable. In this chapter, we'll explore the best kid-friendly activities in Berlin, including top attractions, festive events, and indoor options to keep your children entertained throughout your stay.

## 8.1 Berlin's Best for Little Ones

### Legoland Discovery Centre Berlin

**Overview**
The Legoland Discovery Centre Berlin is an indoor attraction designed to inspire and entertain children with its interactive Lego-themed exhibits. Located in the heart of Berlin, this attraction offers a world of creativity and fun, making it a must-visit for families with young kids.

**Attractions and Activities**

- **Lego Building Zones**: Children can unleash their creativity in various Lego building areas, constructing everything from cars to castles.

There are also themed building challenges and interactive play areas.

- **Miniland Berlin**: A highlight of the centre is Miniland, where iconic Berlin landmarks are recreated in miniature form using Lego bricks. This is a great way for kids to learn about Berlin's famous sites in a fun and engaging manner.
- **Lego 4D Cinema**: The 4D cinema provides an immersive experience with Lego-themed short films, complete with special effects like wind, water, and motion seats.

**Tips for Visiting**

- **Purchase Tickets in Advance**: To avoid long lines, consider purchasing tickets online ahead of time. The centre can be quite busy, especially during the holiday season.
- **Check the Calendar**: The centre often hosts special events and themed days. Check their calendar before your visit to make the most of any additional activities.

**Labyrinth Kindermuseum**

**Overview**

Labyrinth Kindermuseum is a hands-on museum designed specifically for children, offering a wide range of interactive exhibits that encourage learning through play. Located in the Mitte district, it provides a unique experience tailored to younger visitors.

**Attractions and Activities**

- **Interactive Exhibits**: The museum features a variety of interactive exhibits, including a "Wonder World" with sensory play zones, a "City" where children can role-play different professions, and a "Labyrinth" with puzzles and challenges.
- **Workshops and Activities**: Regular workshops and special activities are held to engage children in creative and educational experiences. These might include art projects, science experiments, or storytelling sessions.
- **Special Events**: During the holiday season, the museum often hosts festive-themed events and activities, providing additional seasonal fun for families.

**Tips for Visiting**

- **Check the Schedule**: Visit the museum's website or contact them in advance to learn about current exhibits, workshops, and special events.
- **Dress Comfortably**: Since the museum involves a lot of hands-on activities, make sure children wear comfortable clothing that is suitable for play.

## FEZ-Berlin Adventure Playground

### Overview

FEZ-Berlin is one of Europe's largest non-commercial cultural and leisure centers for children, offering a diverse range of activities and play areas. Located in the Marzahn-Hellersdorf district, FEZ-Berlin is an expansive space dedicated to family fun.

### Attractions and Activities

- **Adventure Playground**: The playground features climbing structures, water play areas, and sandboxes. It's designed to be engaging and stimulating for children of all ages.
- **Indoor Fun**: Inside, there are various activity rooms and play areas, including a space for creative workshops and an indoor climbing wall.
- **Seasonal Events**: FEZ-Berlin hosts a variety of seasonal events, including Christmas markets, puppet shows, and theatrical performances, which are perfect for adding a festive touch to your visit.

### Tips for Visiting

- **Plan Ahead**: Check the FEZ-Berlin website for information on opening hours, admission fees, and any special events happening during your visit.
- **Pack Snacks**: While there are dining options available, packing snacks and drinks for your

children can be a convenient option, especially if you plan to spend the whole day there.

## 8.2 Festive Events for Families

### Santa's Grotto at Alexa Shopping Center

**Overview**
Santa's Grotto at the Alexa Shopping Center is a magical experience for children and families, offering a festive and interactive environment where kids can meet Santa Claus and enjoy holiday-themed activities.

**Attractions and Activities**

- **Meet Santa Claus**: Children can meet Santa Claus, take photos, and share their Christmas wishes. Santa's Grotto is beautifully decorated to create a magical atmosphere.
- **Christmas Crafts**: The grotto often features craft stations where children can make holiday decorations or gifts.
- **Festive Entertainment**: Enjoy live performances, storytelling, and other entertainment that adds to the festive spirit of the event.

## Tips for Visiting

- **Arrive Early**: To avoid long waits, try to arrive early or check if you can book a time slot in advance.
- **Bring a Camera**: Capture the moment with photos of your children meeting Santa and participating in the various activities.

## Children's Christmas Choir at Berliner Dom

### Overview

The Berliner Dom, Berlin's impressive cathedral, hosts a beautiful Christmas concert featuring a children's choir. This event offers a cultural and musical experience that can be enjoyed by the entire family.

### Attractions and Activities

- **Choir Performance**: Listen to the enchanting voices of the children's choir as they perform traditional Christmas carols and festive music.
- **Cathedral Visit**: Explore the stunning architecture of the Berliner Dom and take in the grand interior, which is especially beautiful during the Christmas season.

### Tips for Visiting

- **Purchase Tickets Early**: Concerts at the Berliner Dom can be popular, so it's a good idea to purchase tickets in advance to ensure you get a seat.

- **Arrive Early**: Arriving early allows you to find good seats and enjoy the cathedral's decorations before the performance begins.

## Christmas Crafts Workshops for Kids

### Overview

Many venues in Berlin offer Christmas crafts workshops where children can engage in creative activities and make their own holiday decorations or gifts. These workshops are a great way for kids to get hands-on experience and create something special for the holidays.

### Attractions and Activities

- **Crafting**: Workshops typically include various crafting activities, such as making ornaments, decorating cookies, or creating festive cards.
- **Guided Instruction**: Experienced instructors guide children through the crafting process, helping them develop their creativity and skills.
- **Holiday Atmosphere**: The workshops are often set in festive environments, adding to the holiday spirit and making the experience more enjoyable.

## Tips for Visiting

- **Check Availability**: Workshops may have limited space, so it's advisable to check availability and book in advance if possible.
- **Dress Appropriately**: Some crafts can be messy, so dressing children in old or easily washable clothing is a good idea.

# 8.3 Keeping Kids Entertained: Indoor Options

### Tropical Islands Indoor Waterpark

### Overview

Tropical Islands is a large indoor waterpark located just outside Berlin, offering a tropical escape with water slides, wave pools, and a range of activities suitable for the whole family. It's a perfect destination for a fun day out, especially if you're looking for an indoor adventure.

### Attractions and Activities

- **Water Slides**: Enjoy a variety of water slides, from gentle slopes for younger children to thrilling rides for older kids and adults.
- **Wave Pool**: The wave pool simulates ocean waves, providing a fun swimming experience.
- **Tropical Beach**: Relax on the sandy beach area or take a dip in the warm water, creating a tropical atmosphere even in the middle of winter.

**Tips for Visiting**

- **Book Tickets in Advance**: Tropical Islands can get busy, so booking tickets ahead of time can help you avoid long lines and secure your entry.
- **Pack Swimwear**: Don't forget to bring swimwear, towels, and any other essentials for a day at the waterpark.

## Sea Life Berlin Aquarium

**Overview**

Sea Life Berlin is an engaging aquarium that offers a chance to explore marine life through interactive exhibits and underwater tunnels. It's a great indoor activity for families, providing educational and entertaining experiences for children.

**Attractions and Activities**

- **Underwater Tunnels**: Walk through underwater tunnels to see fish, rays, and sharks up close.
- **Interactive Displays**: Participate in interactive exhibits where children can learn about marine life and conservation.
- **Aquarium Shows**: Enjoy informative shows and feeding sessions that highlight the aquarium's diverse sea creatures.

**Tips for Visiting**

- **Purchase Tickets Online**: To save time and avoid queues, purchase tickets online before your visit.
- **Plan Your Visit**: Check the schedule for feeding times and special events to make the most of your visit.

## Planetarium Berlin's Winter Sky Shows

**Overview**

The Planetarium Berlin offers captivating winter sky shows that provide an educational and visually stunning experience for families. The shows often include fascinating presentations about the stars, planets, and constellations.

**Attractions and Activities**

- **Star Shows**: Watch immersive shows that explore the night sky and the wonders of space.
- **Interactive Exhibits**: Explore interactive exhibits that enhance your understanding of astronomy and space science.
- **Educational Experience**: Learn about the winter constellations and other celestial phenomena in a fun and engaging way.

## Tips for Visiting

- **Check the Schedule**: Planetarium shows have specific times, so check the schedule and book tickets in advance if necessary.
- **Arrive Early**: Arriving early will give you time to find seating and explore any additional exhibits before the show starts.

Berlin offers a wealth of family-friendly activities and attractions, making it an ideal destination for a holiday visit. From interactive museums and festive events to indoor adventures and winter activities, there is something to captivate and entertain children of all ages. By exploring these attractions, you can ensure a fun and memorable trip for the entire family, creating cherished holiday experiences in the vibrant city of Berlin.

# Chapter 9: Unforgettable Day Trips from Berlin

Berlin's festive charm is undeniable, but its surrounding regions offer equally enchanting experiences during the holiday season. Exploring nearby cities and picturesque landscapes can enrich your trip with additional memories and new discoveries. This chapter delves into three exceptional day trips from Berlin, each offering its unique Christmas magic and winter attractions: Potsdam, Dresden, and the Harz Mountains.

## 9.1 Christmas in Potsdam

### Sanssouci Palace in Winter

### Overview

Sanssouci Palace, located in Potsdam just a short train ride from Berlin, is renowned for its stunning rococo architecture and beautifully landscaped gardens. In winter, the palace transforms into a picturesque winter wonderland that offers a serene and enchanting experience.

### Attractions and Activities

- **Palace Tours**: Explore the opulent rooms and exquisite interiors of Sanssouci Palace. During the winter season, the palace's elegant halls, adorned with festive decorations, provide a warm and inviting atmosphere.

- **Winter Gardens**: The surrounding gardens, though less vibrant in winter, still offer a peaceful stroll. The frosted trees and serene landscape create a tranquil setting perfect for winter walks.
- **Special Exhibitions**: Check for any special winter exhibitions or events that might be taking place during your visit. These can offer deeper insights into the palace's history and its role during the holiday season.

### Tips for Visiting

- **Book Tickets in Advance**: To avoid long queues, especially during peak holiday periods, consider purchasing your tickets online.
- **Dress Warmly**: The weather can be chilly, so be sure to dress warmly when exploring the gardens and outdoor areas.

### Potsdam Christmas Market

### Overview
The Potsdam Christmas Market is a charming holiday market set in the heart of Potsdam. Located around the historic Brandenburg Gate and throughout the city center, this market is known for its festive atmosphere and beautiful setting.

### Attractions and Activities

- **Stalls and Stands**: Browse the numerous stalls offering handcrafted goods, holiday decorations, and unique gifts. The market is renowned for its high-quality crafts and artisanal products.

- **Seasonal Delights**: Sample traditional Christmas foods and drinks, such as mulled wine (Glühwein), roasted chestnuts, and gingerbread cookies. The variety of food options adds to the market's festive ambiance.
- **Entertainment**: Enjoy live performances, including Christmas carols and local music, which enhance the market's festive spirit. Children can also enjoy special entertainment, such as carousel rides and storytelling.

## Tips for Visiting

- **Visit Early or Late**: To avoid the crowds, consider visiting the market either early in the day or later in the evening.
- **Cash and Cards**: While many vendors accept cards, it's always a good idea to carry some cash for smaller purchases and stalls.

## A Stroll Through the Dutch Quarter

### Overview
Potsdam's Dutch Quarter (Holländisches Viertel) is a unique area characterized by its red-brick architecture and charming atmosphere. It's an ideal spot for a leisurely stroll, offering a blend of history and modern holiday cheer.

**Attractions and Activities**

- **Historic Architecture**: Explore the distinctive Dutch-style buildings that date back to the 18th century. The architecture, with its gabled facades and narrow streets, provides a picturesque setting.
- **Boutiques and Cafés**: The Dutch Quarter is home to a variety of boutiques, cafés, and restaurants. Enjoy a cup of hot chocolate or a meal at one of the cozy establishments while soaking in the holiday ambiance.
- **Festive Decorations**: During the Christmas season, the Dutch Quarter is beautifully decorated with lights and ornaments, adding to its charm.

**Tips for Visiting**

- **Take a Guided Tour**: Consider joining a guided tour to learn more about the history and significance of the Dutch Quarter.
- **Explore on Foot**: The area is best explored on foot, allowing you to fully appreciate the architecture and festive decorations.

# 9.2 Exploring Dresden's Christmas Charm

## Striezelmarkt: Germany's Oldest Christmas Market

### Overview

Dresden's Striezelmarkt, established in 1434, is one of Germany's oldest and most famous Christmas markets. Held in the historic Altmarkt square, it offers a festive experience rich in tradition and charm.

### Attractions and Activities

- **Historical Stalls**: Wander through the market's historical stalls, offering a wide range of handcrafted gifts, traditional ornaments, and festive decorations.
- **Food and Drink**: Sample traditional Saxon Christmas treats, such as Stollen (a fruit bread), roasted nuts, and sausages. Don't miss the opportunity to try a cup of Dresdner Glühwein.
- **Festive Performances**: Enjoy live performances, including choral music and theatrical performances, which enhance the market's historical and festive atmosphere.

### Tips for Visiting

- **Arrive Early**: The market can get crowded, so arriving early can help you avoid the busiest times and enjoy a more relaxed experience.

- **Warm Clothing**: Dress warmly, as the market is outdoors and the weather can be quite cold.

## Semperoper Dresden's Holiday Performances

### Overview
The Semperoper Dresden is renowned for its stunning architecture and world-class performances. During the holiday season, the opera house hosts a range of festive performances that add a touch of cultural elegance to your visit.

### Attractions and Activities

- **Holiday Performances**: Attend a holiday performance, which may include operas, ballets, or classical concerts. The Semperoper's productions are known for their high quality and festive spirit.
- **Guided Tours**: If you're not attending a performance, consider taking a guided tour of the opera house. The tours offer insights into the building's history and architecture.

### Tips for Visiting

- **Book in Advance**: Tickets for performances can sell out quickly, so it's advisable to book in advance to secure your seats.
- **Dress Code**: For performances, a smart dress code is typically expected, adding to the formal and festive atmosphere of the evening.

## A Winter Walk Along the Elbe River

### Overview

The Elbe River provides a scenic backdrop for a winter walk in Dresden. The riverbanks, especially around the Altstadt (Old Town) and Neustadt (New Town) areas, offer picturesque views and a peaceful retreat from the busy market scenes.

### Attractions and Activities

- **Scenic Views**: Enjoy the winter landscapes and the beautiful views of Dresden's historic buildings along the river. The skyline, with its baroque architecture, looks especially striking against a winter backdrop.
- **Riverfront Cafés**: Stop by one of the riverfront cafés for a warm drink and a relaxing break while taking in the views.

### Tips for Visiting

- **Dress Warmly**: Ensure you're dressed warmly for the walk, as temperatures can be quite low.
- **Check the Weather**: Winter weather can vary, so check the forecast before heading out to ensure a pleasant experience.

## 9.3 A Winter Escape to the Harz Mountains

**Riding the Brocken Railway in the Snow**

**Overview**

The Harz Mountains, located a few hours from Berlin, offer a magical winter escape. The Brocken Railway, also known as the Harz Narrow Gauge Railway, provides a unique way to experience the winter landscape of the region.

**Attractions and Activities**

- **Scenic Train Ride**: Take a ride on the Brocken Railway, which offers stunning views of the snow-covered landscapes and forests. The train journey is a nostalgic and scenic experience.
- **Brocken Summit**: At the summit, enjoy panoramic views of the surrounding snow-covered peaks and valleys. The Brocken is the highest peak in the Harz Mountains, offering a spectacular winter vista.

**Tips for Visiting**

- **Check Schedules**: The railway operates on a specific schedule, so be sure to check the timetable in advance and plan your visit accordingly.

- **Warm Clothing**: Dress warmly for the cold weather and potential snow, especially if you plan to spend time at the summit.

## Christmas in Quedlinburg's Medieval Town

### Overview
Quedlinburg, a UNESCO World Heritage site, offers a charming medieval setting for experiencing Christmas. The town is renowned for its well-preserved architecture and festive holiday atmosphere.

### Attractions and Activities

- **Medieval Christmas Market**: Explore the medieval Christmas market, which features traditional crafts, seasonal foods, and festive decorations. The market's setting in the historic town square adds to its enchanting atmosphere.
- **Historic Architecture**: Wander through the cobblestone streets and admire the medieval half-timbered houses and historic buildings that make Quedlinburg a picturesque destination.
- **Guided Tours**: Take a guided tour to learn more about the town's history and architectural heritage.

### Tips for Visiting

- **Explore on Foot**: Quedlinburg's historic center is best explored on foot, allowing you to fully appreciate its medieval charm.

- **Book Accommodations**: If you plan to stay overnight, consider booking accommodations in advance, as the town can get busy during the holiday season.

### Skiing and Snowboarding in Wurmberg

### Overview

For those looking for winter sports, the Harz Mountains offer skiing and snowboarding opportunities at Wurmberg, the largest ski resort in the region. It's a great destination for outdoor enthusiasts and families looking to enjoy winter activities.

### Attractions and Activities

- **Ski Slopes**: Wurmberg features a range of ski slopes suitable for different skill levels, from beginners to advanced skiers.
- **Snowboarding**: The resort also caters to snowboarders with designated areas and terrain parks.
- **Winter Activities**: In addition to skiing and snowboarding, Wurmberg offers other winter activities, such as tobogganing and snowshoeing.

### Tips for Visiting

- **Check Conditions**: Snow conditions can vary, so check the weather forecast and snow reports before heading to the resort.

- **Equipment Rental**: If you don't have your own equipment, rental options are available at the resort.

# Conclusion

As you wrap up your exploration of Berlin at Christmas, it's clear that this vibrant city offers an unparalleled holiday experience. With its festive markets, dazzling lights, rich cultural offerings, and array of winter activities, Berlin transforms into a magical winter wonderland, making it an ideal destination for a memorable holiday adventure. This guide has walked you through the myriad of experiences that Berlin has to offer during the Christmas season, from enchanting markets and spectacular light displays to delightful dining options and unforgettable day trips.

## Making the Most of Your Berlin Christmas Adventure

To fully embrace the spirit of Berlin during the Christmas season, consider these final tips and recommendations to ensure your trip is both enjoyable and stress-free.

### 1. Embrace the Local Culture

Berlin's Christmas markets, such as those at Gendarmenmarkt and Charlottenburg Palace, offer a taste of traditional German holiday cheer. Immerse yourself in the local culture by sampling regional foods like bratwurst and Lebkuchen, and participating in festive activities such as ice skating and attending seasonal performances. Don't hesitate to engage with locals and learn about their holiday traditions, which can add a personal touch to your experience.

## 2. Explore Beyond the Main Attractions

While the iconic markets and light displays are certainly highlights, Berlin's true charm often lies in its hidden gems. Venture to alternative and themed markets like the Eco-Friendly Market at Kollwitzplatz or the LGBTQ+ Christmas Avenue at Nollendorfplatz. Additionally, exploring neighborhoods such as Prenzlauer Berg and Kreuzberg will provide a more authentic glimpse into Berlin's diverse and dynamic cultural scene.

## 3. Take Advantage of Day Trips

Berlin's proximity to charming nearby cities and scenic landscapes makes it an excellent base for day trips. Consider visiting Potsdam for its winter palace experience, exploring Dresden's historic Christmas market, or enjoying winter sports in the Harz Mountains. Each of these destinations offers a unique perspective on the holiday season and can greatly enhance your overall trip.

## 4. Stay Organized and Plan Ahead

Berlin's bustling Christmas season can be overwhelming, so planning ahead is crucial. Make reservations for popular attractions and performances in advance to avoid disappointment. Keep track of opening hours for markets and museums, and be aware of any special events or closures that might affect your plans. A well-organized itinerary will help you make the most of your time in Berlin and ensure a smoother travel experience.

### 5. Capture the Moments

The festive atmosphere in Berlin provides countless opportunities for memorable photos. Capture the magic of the Christmas markets, the brilliance of the holiday lights, and the joy of seasonal activities. Don't forget to share your experiences with friends and family through social media or a travel journal, preserving the memories of your Berlin Christmas adventure.

## Final Packing Checklist

To ensure you're well-prepared for your Berlin Christmas adventure, use this packing checklist as a guide:

### 1. Warm Clothing

- **Coat:** A warm, insulated coat suitable for cold weather.
- **Layers:** Sweaters, thermal tops, and long-sleeve shirts for layering.
- **Scarves, Gloves, and Hats:** Essential for staying warm while exploring outdoor markets and attractions.
- **Boots:** Waterproof and insulated boots for navigating snowy or wet conditions.

## 2. Travel Essentials

- **Passport and ID:** Ensure you have your passport, visa (if required), and any necessary identification.
- **Travel Insurance:** A comprehensive travel insurance policy to cover any unexpected events.
- **Tickets and Reservations:** Printed or digital copies of tickets for attractions, performances, and transportation.
- **Cash and Cards:** Both local currency (Euros) and credit/debit cards for purchases.

## 3. Electronics

- **Camera:** For capturing the festive lights, markets, and other memorable moments.
- **Smartphone and Charger:** Essential for navigation, communication, and emergency situations.
- **Portable Power Bank:** To keep your devices charged throughout the day.

## 4. Health and Hygiene

- **Medications:** Any personal medications you may need, along with a basic first aid kit.
- **Hand Sanitizer and Masks:** For hygiene and protection, especially in crowded areas.
- **Travel-sized Toiletries:** Shampoo, conditioner, and other essentials in travel-sized containers.

### 5. Comfort Items

- **Travel Pillow and Blanket:** For added comfort during flights or train rides.
- **Reusable Water Bottle:** To stay hydrated while exploring the city.
- **Snacks:** Pack some snacks for the journey or between meals.

### 6. Miscellaneous

- **Map or Guidebook:** A physical or digital guide to help you navigate Berlin and its surroundings.
- **Umbrella:** For unexpected rain or snow showers.
- **Travel Journal:** To document your experiences and reflections during the trip.

## Resources for Further Exploration

To enhance your understanding and enjoyment of Berlin's Christmas offerings, consider utilizing these resources:

### 1. Official Tourism Websites

- **Visit Berlin:** The official tourism website provides comprehensive information on attractions, events, and travel tips. Visit Berlin

## 2. Travel Guides and Apps

- **Lonely Planet Berlin:** A trusted source for detailed travel information and recommendations. Lonely Planet Berlin
- **TripAdvisor:** User reviews and ratings for attractions, restaurants, and hotels. TripAdvisor Berlin

## 3. Local Event Listings

- **Berlin Events:** A platform for up-to-date information on local events, including Christmas markets and performances. Berlin Events
- **Eventbrite Berlin:** Find tickets and information on various holiday events and activities. Eventbrite Berlin

## 4. Cultural Insights

- **Berlin History:** Gain insights into Berlin's rich history and cultural heritage. Berlin History
- **German Traditions:** Learn more about German Christmas traditions and customs. German Traditions

## 5. Transportation and Navigation

- **Berliner Verkehrsbetriebe (BVG):** Information on public transportation in Berlin, including routes and schedules. BVG

- **Deutsche Bahn:** For train travel and schedules within Germany and beyond. Deutsche Bahn

## 6. Dining and Shopping

- **Michelin Guide Berlin:** Recommendations for top dining establishments in Berlin. Michelin Guide Berlin
- **Berlin Shopping Guide:** Explore the best shopping destinations and boutique stores. Berlin Shopping Guide

In conclusion, Berlin offers a dynamic and multifaceted Christmas experience, blending traditional festivities with modern attractions. By utilizing this guide and the resources provided, you'll be well-equipped to make the most of your holiday adventure in Berlin. Whether you're marveling at the festive lights, indulging in seasonal treats, or embarking on exciting day trips, Berlin promises a holiday experience that will leave you with cherished memories and a desire to return.

Made in the USA
Monee, IL
10 November 2024

69781842R00087